How Standards Rule the World

NEW HORIZONS IN ORGANIZATION STUDIES

Books in the New Horizons in Organization Studies series make a significant contribution to the study of organizations and the environment and context in which they operate. As this field has expanded dramatically in recent years, the series will provide an invaluable forum for the publication of high-quality works of scholarship and show the diversity of research on organizations of all sizes around the world. Global and pluralistic in its approach, this series includes some of the best theoretical and analytical work with contributions to fundamental principles, rigorous evaluations of existing concepts and competing theories, stimulating debate and future visions.

Titles in the series include:

Career Dynamics in a Global World
Indian and Western Perspectives
Edited by Premarajan Raman Kadiyil, Anneleen Forrier and Michael B. Arthur

How Standards Rule the World
The Construction of a Global Control Regime
Ingrid Gustafsson

How Standards Rule the World

The Construction of a Global Control Regime

Ingrid Gustafsson

SCORE, Stockholm University, Sweden and SCANCOR, Stanford University, USA

NEW HORIZONS IN ORGANIZATION STUDIES

Edward Elgar
PUBLISHING

Cheltenham, UK • Northampton, MA, USA

Published by
Edward Elgar Publishing Limited
The Lypiatts
15 Lansdown Road
Cheltenham
Glos GL50 2JA
UK

Edward Elgar Publishing, Inc.
William Pratt House
9 Dewey Court
Northampton
Massachusetts 01060
USA

A catalogue record for this book
is available from the British Library

Library of Congress Control Number: 2020933648

This book is available electronically in the **Elgar**online
Business subject collection
DOI 10.4337/9781788975025

ISBN 978 1 78897 501 8 (cased)
ISBN 978 1 78897 502 5 (eBook)
Printed and bound by CPI Group (UK) Ltd, Croydon, CR0 4YY

Contents

Acknowledgements

I am grateful for the financial support, without which this research would not have been possible, from Handelsbankens forskningsstiftelser (P2017-0140:1), the Swedish Research Council (2017-01284), SCORE (Stockholm Center for Organizational Research) and Gothenburg University/School of Public Administration.

1. Organizing a global world

It seems as if the world is becoming increasingly borderless. Products, organizations and services are becoming more and more global in nature, buying products made outside the buyer's immediate environment has become commonplace, and organizations that operate all over the world are becoming the norm. The line between local and global is becoming less distinct, as the borderless world expands, opening the way for a range of product offerings and job opportunities. Few people in the West can picture a world without these global streams of impressions, images, things, products and relationships that flow through our everyday lives.

But globalization also raises questions. Several aspects of products and their production complicate matters and create uncertainty among consumers. It is often difficult to find out how a product is made or whether it poses risks to safety, health, or to the environment. Is this a good product? Will it last? Was child labor used in its production? Are the products safe to use?

Given globalization, a buyer often has no way of asking the producer these questions, since the distances may be great and production sites located far from the consumer. A product may be made in one country, packaged in another, imported to a third country, then sold in yet another. Products and product information are, in addition, becoming increasingly complex. Many are composed of numerous different parts transported back and forth across borders before finally being assembled and sold to someone, somewhere in the world. Making a purchase today can therefore be fraught with uncertainty about the product's manufacture, risks, and characteristics.

This raises a problem. As consumers, we all want to be as certain as we can that the products that we buy are safe, of good quality, and sustainable. At the same time, it is unrealistic to expect each buyer to track each and every part that goes into a product, as well as to monitor and control its production, risks, and product characteristics. One way to reduce this uncertainty is to have someone else separate the good products from the less good, to let others conduct the controls for us. The problems of uncertainty caused by globalization set the stage for a new actor to enter: the third party.

AN 'OTHER'

How to organize such third parties varies across countries and over time. But either way, such uncertainty-reducing third parties should preferably have a degree of authority that instils confidence and trust – someone we can trust other than ourselves. In the past, one common solution for distinguishing good products from bad was for the state to serve as the third party. Using Sweden as a case in point, up until the 1990s, the Swedish state monitored and controlled a large number of products, production facilities and organizations. Its task was to safeguard the public good, to provide a guarantee that products did not pose risks to safety, health, or property. Control of products and production facilities was thereby a responsibility that was assigned to the public sector and was *not* to be managed by commercial enterprises driven by profit. State regulations set out what should be under state control and how the controls should be carried out.

In Sweden, being a country where citizens traditionally have a relatively high confidence in the state's conduct, the state has often served as an 'other,' the third party. State organizations conducted controls on behalf of the country's citizens when citizens were unable to carry out these controls themselves. State monitoring and control is often called 'surveillance' and is something that is taken for granted in society today – that schools, care facilities, workplaces, the gambling market, agriculture, the food sector, and public health are working as they should. What is being put under state surveillance is ultimately a political question – in some countries state surveillance covers a larger number of sectors than in others.

State surveillance also means that parliaments and governments have been responsible for the monitoring and controls carried out. Just as in other sectors where parliament legislates and government governs, surveillance and control form part of a democratic chain of clear command and assignment of accountability. Politicians have thus borne the ultimate responsibility for these control activities.

But big changes have taken place in society since the 1980s. The state is no longer seen as the self-evident 'other' to conduct controls on behalf of the country's citizens. One such changed view of the state's role as a controlling third party relates to substantial changes in how the public sector is organized. Marketization processes (where activities are expected to operate according to a logic of competition) and privatization processes (where public operations are sold and turned into companies or corporations) have reshaped the roles and tasks of public authorities. Companies are, to an increasing extent, now performing tasks that were once performed by public bodies, a process that is sometimes labeled 'NPM' (New Public Management).

Who can, may or should be this third party is also influenced by the fact that people now travel, work and consume across borders. Globalization constitutes an obstacle to carrying out state control as it used to be carried out. National authorities do not have the ability to conduct controls in other countries and on other continents. More and more trade also occurs online, rendering physical and territorial boundaries even more difficult to maintain.

The role of the state is changing, globalization is increasing, and products and production processes are becoming more and more complex. Higher and higher demands are also being placed on products and manufacturing. Other aspects on production processes such as work environment, health, human rights, quality and efficiency are also expanding, placing new requirements on a growing number of organizations, regardless of where the products are being made or the services being sold.

But as our surroundings change, the need for control does not appear to be falling; rather, it appears to be rising. The larger the world around us becomes through globalization, the greater the need for an 'other,' a third party to monitor and control on behalf of citizens and consumers. And if the state is no longer going to be that 'other' – who, then, will be?

One option would be to create a giant global super-organization that monitors and controls all of the world's products. A worldwide 'other.' Such an organization, a power above all powers, could establish the rules for how controls should be carried out, and then itself ensure that these rules are followed. This would mean that all products and production in the world would be monitored and controlled by the same organization, according to the same rules. But it is unclear where such an organization would be situated and who would make the decisions in that organization. It is also unclear what relationship the global organization would have to national governments. There is little incentive for all of the world's product companies to fall in line under a single regulatory organization. An organization of such proportions would likely end up becoming either Orwellian in power or watered down and ineffectual.

Another alternative would be to dispense completely with the third party and have, instead, consumers buy only things that they themselves can assess – by seeing, touching, smelling, and trying them out – with no third-party rules and controls. Quite the opposite of a global super-organization in charge of everything. Consumers would buy products where they are produced, a scenario that reduces uncertainty through local production and direct personal contact. This would negate the need for common rules for monitoring and control, since consumers themselves would decide what is good and what is not. Making purchases in such a situation would be time-consuming, however, as every product would need to undergo the consumer's own sensory controls, which in turn would require that, for every product purchased, buyers would have to make their way to where the product is produced to meet the person who made it. In today's society, few consumers have time for this.

In this book I examine one system that has emerged to control products and organizations, a system with rules for how controls should be carried out and for how products should be designed and work. Millions of organizations follow these rules so that their products and activities can be compared and coordinated, and thousands of organizations are working to ensure that the rules are followed. In the book I call this system a 'global control regime,' a *regime* being a control system, an order built specifically to govern.

The global control regime has been created to control people, organizations, and products. In this regime, the 'other' is not an authority of the local state but a certification company operating on a market, and the rules used to control are not established by the local parliament, but standards set by international standardization organizations. Over the past 30 years, the global control regime has grown and become nested in both the private and public sectors; a development that has occurred in silence, without debate – in research, politics, or the media – despite the fact that the global control regime affects the work of companies, state authorities and consumers every day. Expansion of the control regime has meant a change in who might be assigned responsibility and who governs. Most people today, however, know little about how the global control regime is constructed, how it came to be, who is in charge, and who is responsible. For this reason, this book sets out to uncover the global control regime.

STANDARDS, CERTIFICATION AND ACCREDITATION

In the global control regime, international standards are used to regulate products and organizations. Creating a standard means creating a rule for measures, dimensions or terminology for something, a common vocabulary to standardize and make things comparable. Related concepts include *formalization, quantification, routinization, evaluation, classification, rationalization,* and *objectification* (Timmermans and Epstein 2010) – processes that enable standardization, coordination and governance. Creating a society with a functioning road system, measurement and weight system, and systems for population registry, registration of ownership, employment and wages, pretty much all aspects of an organized society, has to do with standardizing and coordinating things to allow them to be governed from a central location (Scott 1998).

In the context of monitoring and control of products and organizations, the term *standard* has been assigned a specific meaning. A standard is a rule that specifies how a control should be carried out, how a product should be designed, or how an organization should be organized. Once established, standards have a curious tendency to become invisible and work unseen in the background, sinking below the visible surface (Timmermans and Epstein 2010), often going unnoticed until they are missing, like when a European plug doesn't fit an American outlet.

Standards are created by standardization organizations. A set of committees with different tasks form the basic internal structure of the standardization organizations. A majority of the representatives on the committees come from industry, a smaller part from public authorities or civil society organizations. Together, committee members come up with the standards. A standard is thus the result of discussions and compromises met in the committee work of these standard-setting organizations (Tamm Hallström 2000).

The initial need for a standard often stems from a need to coordinate industrial production between countries (Tamm Hallström 2000; Erlingsdottir and Lindberg 2005), for example, the need for a bolt produced in one country to fit a nut produced in another. But standards are also used in a growing number of areas – everything from tools and machinery to work environments, human rights, and sustainable fishing practices. Since the post-war era, the development of standards, or the 'world of standards' as Brunsson and Jacobsson (2000) called it, has increased in scope:

> When things don't work as they should, it often means that standards are absent. But when ISO-standards are applied, life is just so much richer.

The above quote is taken from an ISO (International Organization for Standardization) video advertisement. At the end of the video ad, the ISO logo appears, the form of which resembles the earth's globe, not unlike the UN logo. The ISO is the world's largest standard-setting organization and creator of the ISO standards used around the globe. The most widely spread of these is the ISO 9001 quality standard, a standard for management systems. ISO 9001 specifies how an organization should establish administrative processes and routines for its day-to-day activities. These processes and routines are documented and written down, according to the standard.

In this context the verb *standardizing* means establishing a standard to be followed. Following a standard is usually voluntary and in this way standards differ from legal statutes or directives (Brunsson and Jacobsson 2000). As opposed to statutory law, a standard is also something that is purchased. For example, the ISO 9001 comes at a cost of approximately 150 USD and is issued as a PDF file upon payment.

International standards are often presented, in research and in practice, as an answer to the questions raised by globalization. Standards constitute a clear expression of a global order and rationalization (Drori, Jang and Meyer 2006). Standards, such as ISO standards, thus constitute a set of common international rules that organizations follow. An increasing amount of the regulatory work earlier handled by nations and states, is now handled by private-law international standards organizations like the ISO or their European equivalents CENELEC (European Committee for Electrotechnical Standardization) or CEN (European Committee for Standardization), and then most often translated and distributed by a national standardization organization. Standardization organizations can be found in a growing number of countries and form an infrastructure that spans the world (Tamm Hallström 2000). The worldwide infrastructure means that the standards apply in a greater number of countries than if they had been set by national parliaments. This is one of the elements symbolized by the ISO globe.

Guillet de Monthoux (1981) described standards organizations as 'rationalization associations,' and the vastly growing standardization as an expression of people's insatiable need to be assured of something, be it safety, quality or just the assurance as such. Standards are intended to create a guarantee of a rational and safe society. They make up a skeletal framework, an infrastructure for a global governance regime, but offer no guarantee that the regime will work. Despite the increased use of standards around the world, the problem of uncertainty remains – we have no way of knowing whether a standard is being followed or not. In fact, a reasonable question would be – why would organizations follow standards at all, if they are voluntary and cost money?

A THIRD PARTY – CERTIFICATION ORGANIZATIONS

In order to ensure that standards are being followed, a third party has been created – namely, certification organizations. It is thus no longer the state, but the certification organizations who are supposed to install trust in products and organizations. Certification is carried out by various certification companies and costs money. It is the organization being certified who bears this cost.

People, products and organizations may become certified. We see the traces of this proliferating control activity through the little signs the certification firms leave behind: logotypes and stamps ensuring that this specific organization or product has passed a control – the Rainforest alliance frog on chocolate bars or the ISO 9001 diploma at the dry cleaners or at the dentist. These logotypes are images aimed to simplify the complexity of a product or organization in order for consumers, customers or citizens to reduce their uncertainty about that product or organization.

We see these logotypes and signs on an increasing number of places because certification is spreading. In 2017, 1.5 million organizations were certified according to ISO standards for management systems (ISO Survey 2017). This means that 1.5 million organizations documented their work routines and showed this documentation to a certification auditor who in turn checked the organization's work against the ISO standard – a costly process in terms of both time and money.

Because it is carried out according to international standards, certification is an international phenomenon in the sense that what it signifies is understood across national borders. This means that a dry cleaner in Nairobi may be certified by the same company as a dentist on the outskirts of Stockholm. Some researchers (Conroy 2007; Bartley 2011; Marx 2011) see the advance of certification as a revolution of sorts. Others (Bromley and Meyer 2015) see it is as a move toward a hyper-organized society.

A LESSER-KNOWN FOURTH PARTY – THE ACCREDITATION ORGANIZATION

In order for a third party to serve its function, one must be able to trust that third party, since it is the third party who makes decisions for us when we, the consumers, don't have the option of direct contact with the producer. While it is true that third-party certification organizations leave a trail after them in the form of labels, symbols and logotypes, to guide consumers and reduce uncertainty, we have no direct contact with the certification company either. As consumers, we are once again left with uncertainty – with no way of knowing whether certification companies are properly controlling if manufacturers are following standards, no way of knowing that certification companies are not being paid to issue certificates without actually setting foot on production sites, and no way of knowing that certification companies are not helping manufacturers to slip through without actually meeting the standards. In other words, certification does not really solve the initial problem of uncertainty.

To handle this unsolved problem of uncertainty, the global control regime has created a fourth party, called 'accreditation.' Accreditation is performed by accreditation organizations, which may be companies or public authorities. Accreditation becomes a control of the controller, a certification of the certifier. Unlike certification, however, accreditation leaves no clear traces for the consumer to see. This may be why the fourth party remains largely unknown, among researchers and practitioners alike. One of the aims of this book is to describe and understand the role of accreditation in relation to standards and certification. Given that accreditation often is constructed as a public task, understanding accreditation also becomes a way of understanding the changing role and function of the state in a global society.

ORGANIZING, ORGANIZATIONS, AND THE MEANING OF 'MACRO-ORGANIZATION'

What I have begun to describe here is a complex global web of standards, standards for standards, control of standards, control of control, and control of the control of control. This vast webbed system appears to be comprised of a large number of organizations that, in different ways, establish the rules, govern, coordinate, and control one another: standards organizations, certification organizations, accreditation organizations, and producers of goods and services. The system is constructed in such a way that it somehow – although spread out all over the world, populated by thousands of organizations – holds together. How?

Organization theory has long inquired about how organizations create coordination and control. Early on, Fayol (1916/2008) and Weber (1922/1983) presented principles of organization and bureaucracy as composed of formalization, coordination, control, authority, regulation and division of labor. In the 1960s, theories of organization gained ground, and the organization as an entity became organization theory's primary unit of analysis (for a detailed description, see Starbuck 2003; Czarniawska 2013): the so-called 'formal organization.' The concept of the formal organization then led to investigations of the organization's environment. Perrow (1986) and Powell and DiMaggio (1991) claimed that organizations are surrounded by other organizations. Concepts such as the 'institutional environment' made up of rationalized rituals (Meyer and Rowan 1977) have been used to understand how organizations adapt and relate to their environment, and the environment has been analysed based on notions of conflicting institutional logics (Friedland and Alford 1991).

In large parts of organization theory, there is an assumption that organizations are influenced, shaped by and adapt to their surrounding environment, a perspective that originated from biology, and inspired by systems theory (Czarniawska 2013). The organization is thereby also assumed to be something separate from its environment (Ahrne, Brunsson and Seidl 2016), something ontologically different.

The global control regime is built by organizations that are organized in a specific way. The regime is thus not a formal organization, but is made up of organizations that organize one another and that together form a complex order. To understand how this order is constructed requires that we widen the scope on organizing, and not reserve it as an activity that takes place only *within* organizations. Orders created *among* organizations must also be understood as organized – controlled, coordinated, governed and regulated. In this book I take an interest in organization theory research that seeks to describe and explain the organizing *of*, *among* and *outside* organizations (Ahrne and

Brunsson 2011, 2019; Czarniawska 2013; Ahrne, Brunsson and Seidl 2016). The imagined line separating organizations and their environment is not a clear or fixed one, but is instead blurred, penetrable, and in constant transformation: the control regime's order is comprised of organization *within, among, outside,* and *of* organizations. The organization created by standards, certification and accreditation, leads to what I describe as 'macro-organization' (see Brunsson, Gustafsson and Tamm-Hallström 2018). In using this term, I put forward a general organization theory argument – that organization as a state of order can be created also among organizations and that organization theory should seek to understand this form of organization through concepts taken from the formal organization and not from its surrounding environment. The theoretical arguments on macro-organization constitute the first contribution of the book, and are elaborated in Chapter 9. Macro-organization is an exceedingly well-organized order that in many ways resembles the formal organization. Just as in the case of the formal organization, macro-organization contains a rationalized hierarchy that builds on rules and documentation, a well-developed division of labor, specialization, coordination, a hierarchy, and centralization. But macro-organization also differs on a number of important points. Macro-organization is built on a large set of formal organizations and organizing efforts between them. As a whole, however, macro-organization has no head – no sovereign, no king, no regent, no boss – no-one in charge with absolute power to decide over all of the participants. Neither is there a rule that, like a constitution, applies for all its parts. This means that macro-organization is an organizational phenomenon in which it is unclear who governs.

WHO GOVERNS?

Previous research on certification and standards has stressed the non-state, market-like characteristics of these activities: certification and standard-setting have been presented as private-law, international, non-state tools for regulation and control in a global world. Concepts such as *non-state market regulation* (Marx 2008) or *non-state market-driven governance* (NSMD) (Bernstein and Cashore 2007) have been used. Standards and certification have also been called a 'social regulatory form' (Bartley 2011), to underline the fact that standards constitute 'soft law,' in contrast to 'hard' technical rules, in practice often national regulations or legislation. Concepts like *system of governance* (Bartley 2007) and *hybrid fields of governance* (Bartley 2011) have also been used to denote the kind of non-state, cross-border organizing that certification and standard-setting represent.

Accreditation is described as a coordinating of standards and certification (Fouilleux and Loconto 2016). Accreditation can be performed by state authorities (Gustafsson and Tamm Hallström 2018), meaning that when it is introduced the picture changes: the state appears to have a role to play in the governance regime, despite its market-like, private law nature. Because accreditation as a topic has escaped scholarly attention, we know very little about how this (often) public hub works in the commercial and market-like setting that standards and certification jointly constitute. Uncovering accreditation and showing how it enables global organizing, is the second contribution of the book.

The global control regime is a phenomenon that diffuses and spans borders. It spans the boundaries between organizations and their surrounding 'environment' as the regime is just as organized among its organizations as within them. The global control regime erases the distinction between local and global – its organizations use the same standards regardless of their location. The boundary between private and public also becomes reshaped. Both companies and authorities work in the control regime – companies follow state laws and authorities follow private-law standards.

But despite emphasizing the boundary-spanning, market-oriented and private-law nature of standardization and certification, previous research elucidates neither the shift that has occurred from public to private in the spread of standards and certification nor the consequences of this shift. Who is responsible for the standards being more and more widely used? Who is responsible for the controls carried out? Who governs authorities when the rules that guide their work come from extra-parliamentary organizations? And what authority do parliaments and governments have to govern given the changes exemplified by the control regime? These are questions that remain to be answered.

The control regime crosses boundaries because it is made up of a large number of standards and organizations organized such that they are held together in a single regime. There is thereby an assumption that the regime is able to govern because it is composed in a certain manner. All of these organizations would otherwise merely constitute a group of organizations. The overarching question in the book is: *How was a global control regime constructed?* By asking how it *was* (and not just how it *is*) constructed, I wish to capture the step-by-step process of how the control regime came to be. All of these organizations, controls and rules have not always been there, but developed over time and continue to grow.

To help answer this, I pose two sub-questions, the first being: *What components were used to build the global control regime and how do these components fit together?*

As noted above, the control regime is made up of several organizations organized in a way that seems to hold the control regime together and allows it to govern. In order to understand and explain how this occurred, I examine which organizations make up the control regime, what they do, who they control, who controls them, what the rules are and how these rules are linked to the different organizations. I call the various parts of the control regime – that together make up its construction – 'components.'

I described above how accreditation organizations represent a fourth party of the control regime. While accreditation may be invisible and remain, to most onlookers, unknown, it is also gaining influence in the control of certification, which should make accreditation a key component in the construction of the control regime. But despite accreditation's importance in the construction of a global control regime, and despite accreditation in many EU member countries constituting a part of the state administration, the body of research on the topic is very limited. It thereby constitutes an interesting area for research on public administration.

In order to understand the workings of accreditation, I also ask *What role does accreditation play in the global control regime?* The focus on accreditation may have to do with the role and responsibility of the state in a global world. Accreditation serves as a lens through which I am able to illustrate what a changing public sector can look like.

In order to study the construction of the global control regime, I needed to collect field data, and I needed a starting point. This starting point was Sweden in the 1970s. As a starting point, it serves as an illustration of how control and testing of products was carried out before the control regime came into being. It also serves as an illustration of how a public order was replaced by a global and mostly private one. The case of Sweden is used as a point of observation, I describe the changes happening in Europe over time, from a Swedish perspective. But as Sweden is a part of Europe, the general changes and reform ideas being presented in the field material are illustrative for other countries as well. As the global control regime emerges, the case of Sweden becomes less and less visible and the regime itself comes into focus.

OUTLINE OF THE BOOK

Following this introductory chapter, Chapter 2 presents a review of earlier research on standards and certification, as well as the small body of research on accreditation.

In Chapter 3, I place standards, certification and accreditation in a theoretical context. I develop my arguments regarding research on organizing within and among organizations, after which I present a framework that enables an analysis of the global control regime as a way of governing at a distance, as well as ideas on the organizing of and among organizations.

Chapters 4 and 5 present the data from my field study. Chapter 4 describes the organization of the testing and control that emerged in Europe and replaced many national testing systems, the so-called 'Global Approach' initiated by the European Union. The Global Approach comprises self-conducted control, certification, standards, market surveillance and accreditation. Chapter 5 describes the Goods Package, a reform of the Global Approach granting accreditation a central function. Chapter 5 closes with a description of the European and international organizations of accreditation that enabled the control regime to become global.

In Chapter 6, I study the components that make up the control regime and the juxtaposition of these components, basing my analysis on the framework presented in Chapter 3.

In Chapter 7, I discuss the analysis in relation to the notions of governing at a distance. I show that the control regime governs by blurring the line between controlling and being controlled – the controller and the controlled are often the same organization. In this way the control regime is also able to absorb distance.

In Chapter 8, I discuss my analysis, present my conclusions, and relate the results of the analysis to previous research on standards and certification, as well as discussing the consequences of the control regime with respect to the role and responsibility of the state.

In Chapter 9, I elaborate and extend the theoretical argument about organizing among organizations, by delving more deeply into the discussion of macro-organization.

2. Standards, certification and accreditation

In this book I ask how a global control regime was constructed, and this chapter is devoted to earlier research on the topic of standards, certification and accreditation. Some questions are guiding the outline of the chapter, such as: What are the characteristics of standards that enable them to serve as international rules? How is the relationship between public regulation and standards described? How does the research describe the function of certification in relation to standards? How has accreditation been described? And does the research hold answers that can create an understanding of how the control regime was constructed?

A SPECIFIC TYPE OF RULE

A standard is a type of written rule with a clearly identified author, the purpose of which is to control how people behave in a given situation. The literature on standards often takes its point of departure in the definition of core features of standards relative to other types of rules. This is done by Brunsson and Jacobsson (2000), for example, who differentiate between standards, norms and directives. From the perspective of new institutionalism, norms are taken-for-granted rules that are followed without the person who follows them consciously thinking about it or making an active decision to follow the norm. Norms are only noticed when they are broken or departed from (Jepperson 1991). Norms are usually not written down because they are internalized in people's behavior. Directives, on the other hand, are written rules with a clear author, often an organization, and the author usually has the authority to attach sanctions to the directive, should it not be followed. Based on this categorization, legal instruments (laws and regulations) can be seen as a form of mandatory directives, and authorities, ministries and governments/parliaments can be seen as their authors.

Standards borrow features from both norms and directives. Standards are written, explicit and, like directives, have a clear author (the standards organization that publishes the standard). Standards have evolved from guiding norms to increasingly formalized rules (Kerwer 2005; Fouilleux and Loconto 2016), but standards are not mandatory and have no sanctions attached, and through this voluntary aspect they more closely resemble norms than directives. Standards have sometimes been called 'technical norms' (Joerges and Czarniawska 1998), but norms are in this case not to be seen as taken-for-granted expectations of patterns of behavior but as a model for technical performance.

In theory, anyone can follow standards and anyone can create standards (Brunsson, Rasche and Seidl 2012), something that is often emphasized when discussing the nature of standards as voluntary rules. Companies, trade associations and other stakeholder groups can all create their own standards that they follow or attempt to get others to follow. Tamm Hallström described a standard as 'a voluntary, generally formulated recommendation, drawn up by a standards organization' (Tamm Hallström 2000: 5). In doing so, she linked the standard to its author: standards are written by specific standards organizations.

Timmermans and Epstein (2010: 71) stressed the formal and explicit nature of standards: 'more or less formal standards, which tend to be those developed and adopted through explicit procedures that historians can trace.' Feng also saw standards as explicit specifications by distinguishing them from 'norms, habits, customs, and other tacitly understood rules of practice' (Feng 2003: 99). Loconto and Busch (2010: 508) wrote that standards 'are the measures by which people, practices, processes and products are judged.' In an *Organization Studies* special issue on standards (2012, Vol. 33, No. 5–6), the following definition was given: 'A standard can be defined as a rule for common and voluntary use, decided by one or several people or organizations' (Brunsson, Rasche and Seidl 2012: 616).

Standards have often also been described as a form of 'social regulation' (Bartley 2007, 2010; Marx and Cuypers 2010; Marx 2011; Sandholtz 2012) or 'soft regulation' (Mörth 2006; Djelic and Sahlin-Andersson 2006). By 'social' here is meant that it is usually stakeholder groups who have created or been involved in the writing of a standard, and that standards regulate social aspects of society such as working conditions or social sustainability. Thus 'social' standards stand in opposition to 'technical' standards, which regulate things such as nuts and bolts (as in technical norms). The term 'soft regulation' refers to the voluntary nature of standards, in contrast to 'hard regulation' such as laws and directives: standards are voluntary best practice rules. In contrast to formal law, standards seek to convince rather than to coerce (Kerwer 2005). The focus of research that describes standards as non-state and voluntary has often been stakeholder groups, as either the followers or creators of standards (see Bartley 2007; Bernstein and Cashore 2007).

Standards are not created by national parliaments or public authorities, but an increasing number of private-law standardization organizations. This means that standards fall under private law and cannot be held under administrative judicial scrutiny (Jacobsson 1993). In addition and in contrast to other types of rules, a person who wants to use the standards created by others must often pay to gain access to them.

Even if definitions and problematizations of standards often stress the private-law nature of standards, this does not mean that, as private rules, standards do not have anything to do with public-law rules such as laws, regulations and other administrative provisions – they are often intertwined and might even refer to each other (at least the public regulation might refer to a standard). As Frankel and Hojbjerg (2007) noted, standards can hardly be seen as 'neutral,' 'hard' instruments, but instead as a way by which to create policy. Bartley (2011) claimed, for example, that standards should be studied in relation to national, public rules, and has criticized the standardization research in which standards are presented as rules used in a vacuum out of reach of the state (cf. Brunsson and Jacobsson 2000), or where standards are presumed to fill a 'policy void' (cf. Bernstein and Cashore 2007).

Thus, standards are a specific type of rule – an explicit, written rule with a discernable author whose aim is to control how people behave in a given situation. Compliance with standards is voluntary, and standards are different from legal instruments such as laws or regulations in that they are not created in national parliaments. In following, neither can they be adjudicated from an administrative law standpoint. The research stresses that standards are often created as a kind of 'social' or 'soft' regulation used where states are unable or not permitted to regulate. At the same time, it is also stressed that standards are not to be viewed as completely separate from public-law regulation, but should be studied in relation to laws and regulations.

Because the global control regime is constructed with standards, it is reasonable to conclude that the control regime is constructed with voluntary, private-law rules that are used where states are unable or not permitted to regulate. But it must also be presumed that standards stand in relation to national statutes in some way.

Standards are, accordingly, explicit rules aimed at controlling behavior in a given situation. But how?

GLOBAL CONTROL THROUGH STANDARDIZATION

The use of the type of standards discussed above began in the manufacturing industry as a solution to the problem of coordination between factories. Driving forces behind this were the world wars and the need for an efficient way of producing war material, which standardization was to help with (Guillet de Monthoux 1981). One of the first international standards emerged during the early 1900s and had to do with nuts and bolts and how they are threaded (Tamm Hallström 2000). Explicit rules that could be followed in different places at the same time were needed. Standards standardize by creating alignment, and thus coordination. A nut produced made in one location must fit a machine made in another.

The literature on standards often gives examples of everyday phenomena that work because they are standardized, in the sense of being coordinated. The term 'ubiquitous' has been used to describe the omnipresence of standards in more and more areas of society (see e.g. Timmermans and Epstein 2010; Loconto and Busch 2010; Brunsson, Rasche and Seidl 2012). At the same time, many researchers claim that standards are something that remain unseen, that people rarely think about or reflect on.

According to Lampland and Star, standardization exists in order to 'streamline procedures or regulate behaviors, to demand specific results, or to prevent harm' (2009: 10), while Timmermans and Epstein describe standardization as a phenomenon that helps to:

> … regulate and calibrate social life by rendering the modern world equivalent across cultures, time and geography (…) [as] a process of constructing uniformities across time and space, through the generation of agreed upon rules. (Timmermans and Epstein 2010: 70 ff.)

Timmermans and Epstein make an important point with respect to how control through standardization is able to function even when there is distance between the controller and the controlled: by aligning and thereby coordinating, people, behaviors and organizations can be controlled across both time and space. This sets standards apart from other types of rules, such as national laws and regulations, whose ability to control is limited to a given territory, sector or jurisdiction.

The use of standards has increased dramatically since the post-war period – the need for standardizing having seemingly intensified in step with the globalization of markets. Loconto and Busch (2010) suggest three driving forces behind the growing use of standards: (1) the need to maintain meteorological and technical measurements, (2) the need to meet consumers' desire to be able to trust products on markets, and (3) the need to facilitate international trade.

Standards are often presented in the context of globalization – as a regulatory tool in an internationalized and marketized world, which has been highlighted in a large number of studies.[1] Several studies discuss standards as a part of globalization and the idea that an increasingly globalized world requires more coordination, control and regulation (Drori, Meyer and Hwang 2006; Drori, Höllerer and Walgenbach 2014). Rasche and Seidl (2019) noted that standards might be particularly favorble as tools for global regulation because many of them are not accompanied by various forms of monitoring.

Brunsson and Jacobsson (2000), and later Bartley (2007) and Fouilleux and Loconto (2016), have noted that because standards are created by international standards organizations, not national parliaments, they are suitable tools for international regulation. These texts also stress international and global coordination as a motive behind the widespread use of standardization:

> ... standards generate a strong element of global order in the modern world, such as would not be impossible without them. People and organizations all over the world follow the same standards. Standards facilitate co-ordination and co-operation on a global scale. They create similarity and homogeneity even among people and organizations far apart from one another. (Brunsson and Jacobsson 2000: 1)

The increasing global trade has often also been argued to be the strongest driver of the expansion of standards (Loconto and Busch 2010; Marx 2013, 2014), and standards have been discussed as a way for industries to coordinate or 'self-regulate' (Haufler 2001, 2003), that is, companies use rules developed and imposed not by the state, but by the industries themselves (Fjeldstad, Snow, Miles and Lettl 2012). Standards have also been studied as a way to coordinate markets. Companies can either work together by following the same standards, or compete by creating new standards and attempting to gain market shares (Farrell and Saloner 1988; Besen and Farrell 1994).

In line with the discussion of standards as a form of self-regulation created by various industry organizations, the research has raised issues that have to do with how authority is created at a global level where there is no equivalent to a parliament in place to create rules and no supervisory authority to ensure that the rules are followed (see e.g. Tamm Hallström 2000; Abbott and Snidal 2009; Bromley and Meyer 2015). When researchers have discussed global governance and the creation of authority, concepts such as *private authority* (Cutler, Haufler and Porter 1999) through non-government organizations (NGOs) have received much attention. *Spheres of authority* (SOAs) (Rosenau 2007) is another concept discussed – in a globalized world, there is no one authoritative center but several different spheres that govern and regulate, in different ways, at the global level.

Standardization accomplishes coordination by bringing things into alignment and making them comparable. Standardization occurs over time and space, across cultural and geographical borders. Through standardization, standards are able to control at great distances: manufacturing processes in one country can be coordinated with manufacturing processes in another. The need for coordinated measurements, dimensions and units, increased international trade, and people's need to be able to trust products, are put forward as key drivers in the expansion of standardization.

From what I just presented, a number of explanations for the emergence of the control regime might be highlighted: standards are used to standardize and coordinate which makes control at a distance possible – via standards, goods produced in one country can be controlled by standards created in a completely different location. Standards seem, quite simply, to be suitable rules to use in a global control regime. But how are standards created and who follows them?

STANDARDS FOR AND BY ORGANIZATIONS

Standards have developed more and more from technical specifications of how physical objects should be constructed to descriptions of how organizations should carry out their work (Joerges and Czarniawska 1998). And although standardization implies something stable and conform, standardization actually involves a great deal of dynamics and variation (Brunsson, Rasche and Seidl 2012) with regard to who writes the standards and who follows them, as well as what is being standardized (see also Lampland and Star 2009). Standards have developed from standardizing physical things to standardizing organizations, and given this redirection of standardization toward organizations, organization theory has shown more and more interest in standards as an organizational phenomenon. The research on standards could be divided into studies of organizations that follow standards and studies of organizations that write standards: 'standardizing of organizations' and 'standardizing by organizations' (Brunsson, Rasche and Seidl 2012).

Standards can be generic or specific. As I mentioned in Chapter 1, the most common type of standards are those of the ISO 9001 series. These standards prescribe how an organization should structure its internal administrative system (Walgenbach 2001). The type of activity the organization is involved in is of less importance, because the procedures specified by ISO 9001 standards are generic. Other standards are more specific – a standard for organic farming, for example, is used in the agricultural sector not by companies in the technology sector (Lampland and Star 2009), even if companies in both of these sectors may use ISO 9001 for their administrative systems. Yet other standards may be generic but have a specific goal, for example SA 8000, which regulates the ethical work of organizations (Gilbert and Rasche 2007). Companies that use SA 8000 may come from different industries, but use the same standard to achieve certain ethical goals.

When the implementation of standards is discussed, the object of study has often been private companies, above all technology firms in industry (Walgenbach 2001; Beck and Walgenbach 2005; Seidl 2007; Boiral 2012; Sandholtz 2012). The issues studied have to do with why and how companies comply with standards and the consequences of standard compliance. Several studies discuss the use of standards with assumptions based in new institutionalism, using the formal organization as the unit of analysis, where concepts such as *decoupling* and *legitimacy* have been important analytical factors (Walgenbach 2001; Beck and Walgenbach 2005; Mendel 2006). Walgenbach (2001) and Beck and Walgenbach (2005) use the concept of decoupling when theorizing how organizations implement standards in their day-to-day operations, but when the use of a standard does not have the intended consequences.

Explanations given for why organizations follow standards in the above-mentioned studies include that standards are followed because of pressure from the environment, that other organizations follow them so even more organizations feel obligated to do the same. Standards are considered to be legitimate and this affords them their power to control (Marx 2010, 2013, 2014). Organizations also use standards to compete with one another, or to create or resolve conflicts with one another (Farrell and Saloner 1988; Besen and Farrell 1994).

Another explanation for why standards are followed is directed toward the standardization organizations themselves: how these organizations are structured plays a role in whether or not the standards are followed. The assumption is that the internal structure of standards organizations matters and, according to these studies, how standards are created is important for understanding the penetrative power of standards in society. International standards organizations are usually organized as member organizations with various committees (Farrell and Saloner 1988). The members are made up of national standards organizations, though companies, industry associations, stakeholder groups and government authorities also take part as members or participate at meetings (see e.g. Boström 2006; Tamm Hallström and Boström 2010; Brunsson, Rasche and Seidl 2012). ISO is the most studied standardization organization. The studies have dealt with ISO's internal organizing, using concepts such as, for example, *authority* (Loya and Boli 1999; Tamm Hallström 2000; Boström and Tamm Hallström 2010). The internal structure of ISO is assumed to give the standards authority, thus also increasing the likelihood of compliance with the standards.

Inclusiveness is another concept discussed in studies of standards organizations (Tamm Hallström 2004; Bartley 2007; Boström and Tamm Hallström 2010). Inclusiveness has to do with who is allowed to participate in the standardization committee work and how. Moreover, organizations access to the committees is created or hindered. Transparency and participation in standards organizations are listed as important factors for standards being viewed as both legimate and effective as regulatory tools (Bernstein and Cashore 2007; Marx 2014). Marx (2013, 2014) stresses the importance of 'the institutional design' in the development of standards, and further, in addition to particpation and transparency, the importance of having a structure for attributing responsibility. Concepts such as *transnational multi-stakeholder standardization* (Tamm

Hallström and Boström 2010) have been used to show that many different types of stakeholders participate in standard creation and that standardization is not bound by territorial borders.

To summarize, one could say that there is a large body of research on the organizations that follow standards and the organizations creating standards. However, despite the fact that the research emphasizes that standards should not be seen as separate from the public sector, studies of organizations that follow standards are conducted almost exclusively on companies and associations. Studies on the use of standards by authorities are lacking.

Organizations comply with standards because they are seen as legitimate, because others comply with standards, to out-compete others who don't comply, and because the standardization organizations are organized in a way that bestows the standards with authority. At the same time, studies show that organizations' compliance with standards is not nearly as extensive as one might expect: concepts such as decoupling indicate that organizations may say that they follow a standard but that their work, in practice, is not affected to the extent dictated by the standard.

In order for standards to work as part of a control regime, components that ensure standard compliance are required. It is time for certification to enter this story.

CERTIFICATION – A FOR-PROFIT CONTROL

There is a growing interest in a closely related phenomenon to standardization, namely certification, the third party that is to make sure that standards are actually followed. Etymologically certification comes from being certain, 'a demonstration of proof,' and so certification has to do with being assured of something.

Certification can mean many things. When someone has completed taking diver's lessons, for example, one is a certified scuba diver. In the control regime, however, certification has a specific meaning: in this context certification refers to a control of compliance with standards (Bartley 2007). Studies on certification constitute an expansion of sorts of the standardization research, even if the certification literature is much less exhaustive than the literature on standards, despite certification often occurring where standards are used. Like standardization, certification is a technique for creating trust between actors separated by great distances (Higgins and Tamm Hallström 2007; Loconto and Busch 2010; Fouilleux and Loconto 2016). Certification has been described as a way to organize in a global world, a description in which stressing the international and non-state nature of certification has been important. A large portion of the research presents certification as a tool for global control and, here, the arguments often resemble those found in the literature on standardization. The point of departure for these studies is usually a specific sector in which certification is used to solve concrete problems and to fill a gap:

> ... products are increasingly produced and traded globally. Developing and newly industrialized countries, often with weak or non-existent environmental, health and safety regulatory frameworks, are becoming major producers of agricultural and industrial products ... as a result, regulatory gaps are occurring. (Marx 2011: 600)

The certification literature accentuates the commercial nature of certification and the certification market appears to be growing (Loconto and Busch 2010; Marx 2011; Fouilleux and Loconto 2016; Gustafsson and Tamm Hallström 2018). Certification is presented as both having arisen out of market forces, as an alternative to state controls, and having emerged from politically pro-pelled negotiations (Bartley 2007, 2011). In studies that view certification as mainly driven by stakeholder groups (Bartley 2007; Bernstein and Cashore 2007), often within the environmental movement (Hatanaka 2010), market forces is analysed as an important driver for the emergence of certification. However, Marx, for example, writes that standards and certification are becoming increasingly legitimate tools for regulation and control because they are used in the public sector as well (despite Marx calling them 'private regulation') (Marx 2011, 2013, 2014). Public administrations use (and thereby recognize) standards and certification in three ways: (1) by seeking certifi-cation themselves, (2) by making certification mandatory in legislation, and (3) by adding certification to the public procurement process (Marx 2010). Early on, Jacobsson (1993) claimed that standards and certification were not at all merely something for private organizations and were in fact extensively used by public administrations, but more recent studies of the phenomenon are lacking and have been called for, for example, by Hatanaka and Busch (2008). Just as in the standardization research, the majority of the certification research, regarding both the certifying and certified organizations, has focused on private-law organizations like companies and associations. Studies on cer-tification in the public sector would appear to be lacking.

CERTIFICATION – MORE ORGANIZATIONS IN THE CONTROL REGIME

As I wrote in Chapter 1, certification serves as the third party with the authority and credibility to choose for consumers when the consumers themselves are unable to choose. One of the assumptions made in the research is that in order for certification to be credible as a control, the certification company should be independent from and impartial in relation to the party being certified. Some studies have been conducted to explain how standards organizations create their own certification standards and associated control mechanisms (Bernstein and Cashore 2007; Tamm Hallström and Boström 2010; Marx and Cyupers 2010; Marx 2013). In this context different forms of certification have been discussed: it has been pointed out that certification can be carried out as first-party, second-party or third-party certification. Marx (2011) described the differences between various forms of certification in more detail: first-party certification is where an organization itself creates some form of standard that the organization then checks itself against. That is, the entire certification process takes place internally. Second-party certification refers to where the same organization that creates a standard then certifies another organization's compliance with that standard. In this case the standards/certification organization is the second party to the party being certified. Because there is, according to Marx, no guarantee of impartiality of the certification in these contexts, he has called this form of certification 'self-regulation.' In *third-party certification*, there are three organizations involved: one that writes the standards, another that does the certifying, and yet another that is certified. According to Hatanaka and Busch (2008), the concept of third-party certification (TPC) signals organizational independence and is the form of certification that has become the most legitimate and considered the most credible (Fouilleux and Loconto 2016; Gustafsson and Tamm Hallström 2018).

One factor in the proliferating market for certification as stressed by Walgenbach (2001) and Boiral (2012), is that certification is performed on a commercial basis, by companies that receive payment from the organizations they certify (cf. Gustafsson and Tamm Hallström 2013). The use of concepts such as impartiality and independence becomes problematic since the certification companies are financially dependent on their customers, that is, the organizations certified. According to Walgenbach, this leads to increased mistrust of certification as a method of control. Studies also show that when standards are not followed in practice, the certification – the guarantee of standard compliance – becomes a mere display window for the surrounding environment, detached from the day-to-day activities (Boiral 2012). If the certification audit becomes a superficial and predictable control, certification creates distrust rather than trust and therefore tends to generate more rather than less control, the latter of which was the original idea behind ISO 9001 (Walgenbach 2001).

The above argument encapsulates an important aspect of the global control regime. According to the above discussion, certification companies should remain independent from the organization being certified, and even from the organization creating the standards. It would appear important that the organizations are separate from one another. This means more organizations are created in the control regime – instead of handling everything within one organization (Marx's 'first-party certification') boundaries are drawn between different organizations: standardization organizations, organizations that follow the standards, and certification organizations. There seems to lie credibility in the idea of 'organizational independence' (Hatanaka and Busch 2008; Kouakou, Boiral and Gendron 2013) between the different organizations involved in the control regime. In addition, the market for certification is growing, leading to growth in the number of certification organizations. This leaves the global control regime with more entities to control.

The research describes how certification is used as a solution for controlling in a global setting, a way of creating trust between organizations that are far apart from each other. It also shows how the growth of certification is driven by commercial market forces, with the researchers stressing that these commercial drivers create an incentive for certification companies to sell certificates without ensuring that standards are followed, something that would undermine the credibility of the certification. With the rising demand for certification services, the number of organizations in the control regime increases even more.

But if certification is driven by commercial forces that might create an incentive to not conduct proper controls of compliance with standards – how, then, can trust be maintained? It is here that accreditation enters the picture.

ACCREDITATION – THE UNKNOWN FOURTH PARTY

The term 'accreditation' has several meanings. Among other things, it can refer to something that journalists need in order to gain admission to and report from a political event, or to something carried out to ensure a certain quality of universities (Wedlin 2011). In the control regime accreditation refers to a control of certification and is carried out on the basis of standards (Marx 2011; Fouilleux and Loconto 2016; Gustafsson and Tamm Hallström 2018). The purpose of accreditation is to guarantee the competence of a certifying organization: 'Accreditation is thus the process by which an authoritative organization gives formal recognition that a particular (usually third-party) certifier is competent to carry out specific tasks' (Loconto and Busch 2010: 511). Unlike certification, accreditation is rarely sector-specific. Accreditation can be carried out by stakeholder groups (Bartley and Smith 2010; Marx 2011) or authorities (Jacobsson 1993; Gustafsson and Tamm Hallström 2018), but also by companies (Fouilleux and Loconto 2016).

Since the 1990s, there seems to be more accreditation organizations around to coordinate the growing infrastructure for standards. In both the literature on standards and that on certification, accreditation has at times been referred to as an additional form of control (Loconto and Busch 2010; Loconto, Stone and Busch 2012; Hatanaka, Konefal and Constance 2012; Hatanaka 2014; Fouilleux and Loconto 2016).

Accreditation is used to infuse credibility to certification, as accreditation is meant to guarantee the independence that a certification firm's legitimacy is assumed to rest on (Marx 2013). Thus Marx mentioned of accreditation but does not analyse the accreditation organizations per se, he talked instead about accredited certification organizations, concluding that 'accreditation systems are sometimes put in place' (Marx 2013: 274).

The studies that do include accreditation are mainly limited to organic farming (for an overview, see Hatanaka, Konefal and Constance 2012). Fouilleux and Loconto (2016) cite a need for more research on accreditation. They conducted a review of various accreditation organizations around the globe, but delve no deeper into accreditation per se. According to Loconto and Busch (2010), accreditation has emerged due to the large and growing number of certification companies, and Fouilleux and Loconto (2016) mention accreditation as a part of an emerging field (for standards), though none of them have analysed accreditation specifically. Hatanaka (Hatanaka, Konefal and Constance 2012; Hatanka 2014) looked at accreditation, but as something that has emerged from certification activities, and the study did not focus specifically on accreditation.

To sum up: Accreditation has emerged as a way to coordinate and to affirm the competence of certification companies and thereby adds yet another type of organization to the control regime. Accreditation can be performed by companies, stakeholder groups or authorities. It seems hard, however, based on earlier research, to draw any conclusions regarding the role accreditation plays in the construction of the global control regime. For that I need to know more about the organization of the control regime.

CONCEPTS THAT DESCRIBE THE ORGANIZATION

The literature uses different concepts to describe the set-up of standards, certification and, at times, accreditation. Marx wrote that 'global markets are increasingly governed by certification systems (CS), which aim to regulate transnational supply chains according to a set of standards' (2014: 401), and Bartley (2007) called standardization and certification a 'system of governance.'

As noted, some of the concepts include accreditation. The concept of multilayered conformity assessment systems (MCAS) (Hatanaka 2014) has been used to define certification and accreditation as a layered system of controls: 'multiple tiers of auditing practices' (Hatanaka 2014). Organizing standards and certification in multiple layers has also been concluded to have a tendency to 'ratchet up,' with an increasing number of competing standards and increased competition between different standards organizations (Bartley 2011; Reinecke, Manning and von Hagen 2012). 'Meta-structures' are then created to organize the increasing number of standards and how they relate to one another: a structure for standardizing standards. Bartley claimed that such ratcheting-up tendencies facilitate 'both greater interconnectedness among certification initiatives and greater homogeneity in their organizational form' (2011: 447) but does not analyse this any further.

Levi-Faur and Starobin (2013) distinguish between certification and accreditation by calling them 'first order-' and 'second order regulatory intermediaries,' thus presenting certification and accreditation as middlemen of sorts. Loconto and Fouilleux (2014) define standards, certification and accreditation as 'interconnected activities' that 'shape the organizational field by defining what one can audit, certify, accredit and standardize,' going on to say that the 'creation of these boundaries is one of the ways to institutionalize an organizational field' (2014: 166), thus viewing standards, certification and accreditation as an emerging institutional field.

In an attempt to help describe and understand standards, certification and accreditation, a number of researchers have tried to establish the concept of a tripartite standards regime (TSR) (Loconto and Busch 2010; Loconto, Stone and Busch 2012; Hatanaka, Konefal and Constance 2012; Hatanaka 2014; Fouilleux and Loconto 2016). Hatanaka (2014) writes that what she called 'multiple conformity assessment systems' are a part of a TSR. These concepts seem to overlap and are descriptive – taking accreditation into account but not explaining the role it plays or why it has that role.

A tripartite standards regime is viewed, in turn, as a form of governance – 'a network-based system of regulation, ideally functioning through processes of exchange and negotiation, rather than a state-led system of regulation' (Loconto and Busch 2010: 511). Such a system can also be described as a 'bricolage of multiple layers of markets' (Fouilleux and Loconto 2016: 9). In a TSR, the line between public and private organizations becomes 'increasingly blurred' (Fouilleux and Loconto 2016: 6), a tendency that Bartley (2011) also drew attention to with his concept of hybrid fields of governance. The TSR-idea is linked to the ideas about the 'RIT'-model – where the R stands for regulatory body, the I stands for intermediary and T stands for the regulatory target (Abbot, Levi-Faur and Snidal 2017; Loconto 2017). From this perspective, standards and standardizers are the 'R's and certification and accreditation are both 'I's and 'T's as they are both intermediaries for regulations (such as ISO standards) and the targets of such standards.

Loconto and Busch (2010), Hatanaka (2014) and Fouilleux and Loconto (2016) used the term 'regime' without defining it. For them, the regime is used to describe the interconnected order that standards, certification and accreditation, together, make up. I use the concept of a *control regime* to discuss the organization of standards, certification and accreditation. *Regime* is a suitable term since it means an authoritative or governing order.

UNDERSTANDING STANDARDS, CERTIFICATION AND ACCREDITATION

Coordination through standardization has evolved from initially being aimed at technical and physical objects, to being directed more and more toward the ideas of the formal organization and organizational processes. Standards are created in standards organizations. Standardization enables control of organizations even if they are at large distances from each other.

Certification is carried out by companies that certify other organizations, as a control of and proof that the organization in question complies with a standard. Certification has been described as having grown out of a need to be able to conduct audits and controls in global markets, and as a tool designed to enable actors far away from one another to trust one another. Accreditation has emerged as a way to coordinate and test the competence of certification, but more than that we still do not know about it.

What I can conclude, is that the control regime is made up of standards and a growing number of organizations that monitor and control one another: standardization organizations, certification organizations, certified organizations, and accreditation organizations. In the research on standards and certification, both organizations that certify and organizations that are certified, as well as standardization organizations and standardized organizations, are analysed. The research shows that standards organizations, certification organizations, and accreditation organizations appear to be separate from each other, and that the idea of organizations as separated units is nurtured by the idea of 'independence.'

Research on standards has taken its point of departure in the idea of the organization as the unit of analysis – the attention having focused on either an organization that uses standards or an organization that creates standards. The same is true of research on certification, which has looked at organizations that certify and those that are certified. At the same time, standardization, certification and accreditation are presented as activities that are organized together, as something interconnected. The literature on standards and certification uses concepts such as certification systems, tripartite regimes, RIT, non-state market-driven systems, and multilayered conformity assessment systems, and describes standardization, certification and accreditation as 'interconnected activities.'

The control regime is made up of various organizations that exist all across the world, and there are millions of them. These organizations are somehow assembled, connected and constitute some sort of order. The control regime thereby seems to have to do not only with organizing within organizations, but also organizing outside organizations and among organizations. In the next step of solving the puzzle of how a global control regime has been constructed – that is, a regime that is constituted by millions of organizations and a complex set of rules, covering the entire globe – I need to look more closely at how organizing outside and among organizations can be understood and explained. I also need a greater understanding of how one can create control at a distance.

NOTE

1. Brunsson and Jacobsson 2000; Tamm Hallström 2004; Beck and Walgenbach 2005; Kerwer 2005; Djelic and Sahlin-Andersson 2006; Higgins and Tamm Hallström 2007; Bernstein and Cashore 2007; Bartley 2007, 2011; Timmermans and Epstein 2010; Marx and Cuypers 2010; Tamm Hallström and Boström 2010; Marx 2011; Brunsson, Rasche and Seidl 2012; Boiral 2012; Reinecke, Manning and von Hagen 2012; Loconto, Stone and Busch 2012; Fouilleux and Loconto 2016; Gustafsson and Tamm-Hallström 2018; Rasche and Seidl 2019.

3. Organizing, organizations and distance

Standards are a kind of rule used to control organizations globally as well as locally. Organizations do not always follow the standards they say they do, and therefore a control of compliance with standards seems to be required. This control is performed by certification companies. Certification companies have an economic incentive and may therefore be suspected – rightly or wrongly – of granting certification without having carried out the necessary control. In other words, certification provides no guarantee that a standard is actually being followed. Another type of organization has therefore been created, the accreditation organization. Very little has been written about accreditation apart from that accreditation organizations are to control and coordinate other organizations in the control regime.

When I use the term 'regime,' I mean something, and order, being assembled and somehow held together. The answer to how this is made possible – how the global control regime actually can be a regime with interconnected parts, at the same time as it is global – must lie in its construction, that is, how it is organized. Hence, the construction of the global control regime must be an organizational inquiry.

The global control regime seems to be made up of different types of organizations – standards organizations, certified organizations, certification organizations and accreditation organizations – each of which has different tasks. One important aspect of the control regime's construction is that the organizations of the regime are not gathered in one place but can be found all around the globe, which complicates their control. A large amount of the research on standards and certification stresses precisely this global or international aspect of these activities. Globality and internationality imply distance – controlling globally means that the controller and the controlled are far away from each other. Despite this, the concept of distance has not been problematized in earlier research on standards and certification (one exception being Higgins and Tamm Hallström 2007). In order to analyse how the control regime has been constructed, I need to understand how control at a distance can be made possible – a control where the controlling entity cannot see, speak or communicate directly with the entity controlled.

Because the control regime appears to be made up of organizations, I begin the chapter with a presentation of how ideas about the formal organization came about, followed by a presentation of ideas about how we can understand the organizing of and among such formal organizations. I argue that the same principles used to describe organizing within organizations can just as well be used to describe the organizing of and among organizations. Thereafter, I present ideas on how control at a distance is made possible. The analytical model then presented constitutes a combination of ideas about the organizing of and among organizations, as well as ideas about control at a distance.

ORGANIZING OF AND AMONG ORGANIZATIONS

Perrow (1991) wrote that we live in a 'society of organizations.' An increasing number of activities and relations in society take place in organizations – the list of organizations that control people's lives in different situations can be long. The control regime can be viewed as an example or expression of such a society of organizations. Standards, certification and accreditation target mainly organizations, not human beings.

THE IDEA OF THE FORMAL ORGANIZATION

In the control regime, organizations are controlled. Standards standardize organizations (Joerges and Czarniawska 1998) through dictating what internal procedures, processes and administrative practices organizations should use. Standards presuppose and build on the notion of the organization (Walgenbach 2001; Beck and Walgenbach 2005; Mendel 2006; Meyer 2014). Research on the ISO 9001 standard, for example, presents standardization as something that 'offers a system of standardization of organizational actors' (Mendel 2006: 137), and the assumption is that management standards constitute a kind of 'formal organizational reform' and that such reforms '[rationalize] organizations as social actors' (Mendel 2006: 142).

An organization's internal routines and internal administration – aspects that standards are meant to control – are what organizational research has come to refer to as the organization's formal structure. In the older structural-functionalist organizational research, the formal structure was assumed to be a rational tool for effectively achieving an organization's goals.

In the new institutionalism idea, the organization's formal structure – its rationality, procedures, formalization, hierarchy, specialization and standardization – is a way of appearing legitimate in the eyes of the surrounding environment. The formal structure is a myth, an idea, a façade, that organizations relate to in a ceremonial manner (Meyer and Rowan 1977). This represents a criticism of earlier organizational research's structural-functionalist assumptions.

The picture of the rational organization painted by the structural-functionalist view also contains the notion of there being, or that there should be, a close connection between the talk, decisions and actions of organizations: that talk and decisions precede action, and that the decisions made are implemented, a picture questioned and disproven by organization researchers (March and Olsen 1976; Rombach 1986; Brunsson 1989). Theoretical concepts such as the decoupling of talk, decision and action help to explain how organizations are able to live up to the idea of the rational and formal organization, at the same time as behaving 'irrationally' (Brunsson 1985). These have been the concepts used by researchers (Walgenbach 2001; Beck and Walgenbach 2005; Sandholtz 2012) to explain why standards are not always followed or why certification does not always represent what it is expected to represent.

The institutionalized idea of a formal organization comes with certain expectations (Meyer and Bromley 2013): they are expected to have a means–end structure, control mechanisms, evaluations, written goals, interim goals, follow-up documentation, accounting systems, annual plans, monthly plans, plans for employees, and plans for different departments. Much work of the organization is put into documenting and clarifying the organization's internal structure, thereby creating a boundary between the organization and its surrounding environment by showing what happens within the organization in relation to what happens outside the organization (Meyer and Rowan 1977).

A formal organization is also expected to have a clearly articulated identity (Brunsson and Sahlin-Andersson 2000): a name, a logo, and a slogan. An organization with a clear identity is also sought to be independent and autonomous, with clear boundaries to its surrounding environment. The organization is sovereign in relation to its environment and its members. The formal organization, as a legal person, can act in its own name. It can own resources, and it can have members that are exchangeable: even if they leave the organization, the organization's identity remains.

The formal organization with a rational inside, with a clear identity, autonomy, sovereignty, a hierarchical order, and boundaries to the outside environment, is also assumed to be able to act (Brunsson 2007). Organizations become 'proper social actors' (Meyer 2010). And just like a physical person, as an actor the organization is assumed to be able to make choices and decisions, to act with intention, to have and pursue its own interests, and to have its own independent will: 'An actor is thus much more agentic – more bounded, autonomous, coherent, purposive, and hardwired – than a person' (Meyer 2010: 3). As an actor, the formal organization can also be assigned responsibility in a way that non-actors cannot. A formal organization – which constitutes a separate legal entity – can be brought to justice and expected to account for its activities, and the formal organization is granted more authority than orders that are not seen as an actor (Brunsson and Sahlin-Andersson 2000).

THE PRINCIPLES OF ORGANIZING

From a new institutional perspective on formal organizations, organizing is an activity assumed to occur primarily *within* organizations. Researchers within the field of new institutionalism have certainly problematized the boundary between the environment and the organization by understanding the organization as heavily influenced by its environment. But regardless of how the organization is theorized, the point of departure is that organizing occurs within organizations. Using this as a starting point, anything outside or among organizations becomes something else than what is within them. It seems that organizing is a process that occurs only within organizations. However, it is the organizing outside and among the organizations in the global control regime that holds the key to the puzzle of how the control regime comes about. So how does one capture and analyse the organizing outside and among organizations, without referring to it as 'the environment'?

The idea of the formal organization has not always existed. At the beginning of the 1900s, 'principles' for organizing were presented by Herni Fayol and Frederick Taylor. But at that time, these basic principles were just principles for specific types of organizing, they were not synonymous to activities in formal organizations. Fayol noted that the principle of a clear division of labor was to 'produce more and better work with the same effort' and that 'results in specialization of functions and separation of powers' (Fayol 1916/2008: 42). The principle of authority and responsibility had to do with the right to give orders and the power to have subordinates follow those orders. The principles of unity of command and centralization were to be achieved through good organization. A hierarchical order would ensure communication – subordinates communicate via their managers. And administration was built on the principle of order – everything in its place. A graphic representation of the organization – what we now call an organization chart – was advocated to facilitate this order and the control of activities (Fayol 1916/2008).

The administrative principles presented by Fayol were directed at industry. Similar principles, adapted for public administration, were called 'principles of bureaucracy' (Weber 1922/1983).

While bureaucracy was presented as a specific form of organizing, its principles of authority (rational, traditional or charismatic, where rational authority is characteristic of bureaucracy), specialization and impartiality among the employees were nothing new, but indeed were widely known principles for how organizing occurred in practice. What Weber did was write about bureaucracy as an unbeatable way of achieving efficiency (Waldo 1961; Perrow 1991).

In a bureaucracy, a rational authority (a belief in rules and the legality of regulations) prevails and this is what makes the bureaucracy an effective and invincible model for organizing (Weber 1922/1983). Over the years, administrative and bureaucratic principles have been described in different ways by researchers such as Fayol (1916/2008), Weber (1922/1983), Thompson (1956), Hall (1963), Blau (1968) and Perrow (1991). The notion of bureaucracy is not about organization*s*, but about principles of organizing, such as written documentation, specialist knowledge and specialization, rationalization of collective actions, division of labor, professionalism, and the elimination of nepotism and rules of thumb, an impartial attitude toward work (Weber 1922/1983), standardization, formalization, specialization and hierarchy (Hall 1963). The impartiality in a bureaucracy is ensured through the administration and its bureaucrats being free from interests (both economic and moralistic) in the cases they handle (Weber 1922/1983).

Neither Weber nor Fayol discussed 'organizations,' but the 'principles of organizing,' giving practical advice rather than theoretical arguments about organizations. Hall discussed bureaucratization as a form of organizing that can occur step-wise in different dimensions, and is not necessarily exclusive to the organization as a unit. It was only later that researchers began to theorize and create models, to describe and make abstractions about the concept of organization (Waldo 1961). One of the driving forces behind this was that a more scientific approach was needed as the science of administration had until then been very practical and normative: 'Administration, public or private, is an applied science ... "Administrative theory" suggests an engagement with the world, a striving after values' (Waldo 1961: 217). Behaviorism enabled researchers to begin to make calculations and put numbers to organizations, and thereby abstract the ideas about them (Simon 1962). Organizations became theoretical units and, as such, legal or immortal persons, entities that survive their members or employees (Starbuck 2003; Lamoreaux 2004). This shift also represents a shift in perspective to one where the formal structures (of organizations) became the focus – the organization as something stable, an entity (Czarniawska 2013).

PRINCIPLES FOR ORGANIZING OF AND AMONG ORGANIZATIONS

I agree with Czarniawska (2010) that using the formal organization as the point of departure for analysis does not capture all the organizing that occurs among organizations:

> Organizing may occur within formal organizations, but it is rarely contained within their borders, and imposing such a frame from the outset ('organizing is a process

taking place in formal organizations') possibly excludes many fascinating new phenomena related to organizing. (Czarniawska 2010: 156)

One way to extricate organizing as an activity from the organization as an entity is to understand organizing as a process (Hernes 2007). Based on the concept of action nets (Czarniawska 2004), organizing can be understood as a process of connections between various actions. Some action nets stabilize and can gradually come to form formal organizations; others lead to collaborations, or to nothing. Compared with traditional theories of formal organizations, the action net perspective offers an opposing view – that organizing creates organizations (and not the other way around):

> From the action net perspective, actions come first; networks come second ... and actors, in the sense of such established and recognized units as formal organizations and associations come third. (Corvellec and Czarniawska 2014: 90)

Another line of reasoning to understand organizing among organizations was presented by Ahrne and Brunsson (2011, 2019). They did not differentiate between organizations as one thing and the environment of organizations as another. Instead, they made a distinction between organization and non-organized orders, and talked about organizing not as a process but as the creation of organization as a specific kind of social order. Founding their arguments on March and Simon (1958/1993) and Luhmann (2005), they suggested that what distinguishes organization from other forms of social orders (such as networks or institutions) is that organization is a decided order – organization builds on decisions. Thus organization is not something that emerges out of unknown forces. Organization can be traced to someone who made a decision.

Ahrne and Brunsson broke organization down into five analytical elements – rules, membership, sanctions, hierarchy, and monitoring. These elements constitute the premises of decisions in formal organizations. Organizations can make decisions about who gets to be a member of the organization, they can decide who decides over whom (hierarchy), they can decide on sanctions and which rules should apply, and they can decide how the organization's activities will be monitored.

According to Ahrne and Brunsson, all of these elements can also be used outside organizations. Organizations can organize other organizations through monitoring, membership or rules, for example. By using the different elements outside organizations, organization – a decided order – is created outside and among organizations as well. What is commonly referred to as the *environment* is rather partially organized.

But organizing can occur in more ways than by rules sanctions, hierarchy, membership or monitoring, and Ahrne and Brunsson give no explanation as to why the particular elements noted should be essential for organizing. To follow through on the idea of eliminating the analytical distinction between organizing within and organizing among organizations (which Ahrne and Brunsson started), all principles of organizing that scholars have presented to describe organizing within organizations should be applicable to understand the organizing of and among organizations. In other words, all principles presented by Fayol and Weber should be applicable to understand both organizing within and organizing outside formal organizations.

This, however, does not mean that the formal organization as the unit of analysis is irrelevant to the understanding of the control regime. I still need to understand how organizations are organized in the control regime, but I need to interpret organizations in a new way: as an object of control rather than as a social actor.

ORGANIZATIONS AS OBJECTS

Interpreted from a traditional perspective where the organization as an entity and a social actor is the analytical starting point, a control regime would be made up of formal organizations, organizations attributed characteristics like independence, autonomy, sovereignty and agency. But why would such independent, autonomous and sovereign actors arrange themselves into a control regime? Rather, each independent, autonomous and sovereign actor should want to create its own standards and certifications, and not submit itself to be controlled by other organizations. Herein lies a contradiction, and I therefore need an interpretation of organizations that enables an understanding of them as parts of a control regime.

Along with the action net perspective comes a non-essentialist idea of the organization: an organization has no core. Organizations can, however, be interpreted, described and understood in different ways. For example, they might be likened to machines, or organic systems. Another interpretation of the organization, in addition to the organization as an actor (Brunsson 2007, Meyer 2010), is that of the organization as a legal person – as a subject in its own right able to make statements and be held legally accountable (Lamoreaux 2004).

The organization can also be interpreted as an artefact, a quasi-object (Czarniawska 2013). As a quasi-object, organizations can be used for the purpose of creating something else, like a tool (Perrow 1991).

In Chapter 1 I wrote that standards standardize organizations. The standardization of organizations and the theorizing of organizations as entities have emerged in parallel during the post-war era. Standards are assumed to enhance the characteristics of an organization that make the organization a separate unit of analysis: autonomy, a clearly rational core and boundaries to the environment. However, here I choose another way by which to understand organizations. Instead of understanding standardization of organizations as something that strengthens them as institutionalized, autonomous and demarcated units, I interpret the standardization of organizations as analogous with standardization of physical objects (see Czarniawska 2013). Organizations can be standardized just like nuts and bolts. Thus they can be seen as tools and components rather than units of analysis. This interpretation brings me closer to an analysis of how organizations can be understood in the control regime – enabling me to include organizations in my analysis, but without having to make them an a priori unit of theorization.

In short: in order to understand the organizing of and among organizations, I make no analytical distinction between organizing within and organizing among or outside organizations. That is, I turn the idea of the formal organization and what has come to be called the 'formal structure' inside-out. The principles of hierarchy, authority, rationalization, creating routines, standardization, formalization, the division of labor, regulation, coherence, centralization, documented processes, coordination, impartiality and specialization are not analytically destined to organize only within organizations. These analytical principles can create an understanding for organizing both within, of and among organizations.

In addition, I understand organizing as a process, and that organizations can be interpreted in different ways, enabling organizations to be interpreted as quasi-objects and tools in the construction of the global control regime, rather than interpreting them as autonomous, sovereign actors.

The control regime is global, meaning that the controlling entity cannot always see, hear or speak with whom or what is being controlled. The organization that creates a standard is not in direct contact with the one that follows the standard, the organization that accredits is not in direct contact with the one that certifies, and so on. The global control regime's organizations and their activities are spread out, spatially, from one another – let's keep in mind that the global control regime comprises millions of organizations. At the same time, the same standards are used all over the world – an organization in Nairobi may follow the same standard as an organization in Kiruna in Sweden's far north, and the organization in Kiruna that follows the standard may actually have more in common with the organization in Nairobi than it has with an organization right across the street from it in Kiruna. In this way standards affect our conceptions of globality and distance.

The organizations in the global control regime are both close to and far away from one another. How is that possible? It is time to dig deeper into theories of how to control at a distance.

ORGANIZING GLOBALLY

Just as the concept of organizing is not restricted to organizations, the concept of distance is not restricted to spatial distance. While distance can refer to the absolute distance between two points, distance can also be cognitive, relational, spatial, temporal or geometric (Law and Hetherington 2000; Sundström 2011; Corvellec, Ek, Zapata and Zapata Campos 2016). According to Law and Hetherington, distance is something created in the assembling of people, objects, time and relations. Distance is an effect, rather than an absolute state.

This idea builds on a view of materiality that differs from conventional social science, where technology and physical things constitute something different from 'the social'. For Law and others in science and technology studies (STS), from which also Latour's (1987, 2005) ideas stem, technology, materiality and sociality are not separate phenomena but create one another. One cannot understand materiality without understanding sociality, and vice versa. People, physical and material things, and technology together create the social.

The view of distance as something created, as an effect rather than an absolute state, implies also that the concept of globality (and globalization) is something relational and relative, as well as practical and material (Law and Mol 2008). If linked to other practices and physical things in other places, a local practice can become global. What we perceive as far away and global one day, may be perceived as close and local the next: 'objects, materials, information, people and (one might add) the division between big and small or global and local, these are all relational effects. They are nothing more than relational effects. Which is why it is so important to study how they are produced' (Law and Hetherington 2000: 38).

Globalization expands the environment of organizations both cognitively and spatially. Earlier research on standards, certification and accreditation have mentioned the concept of distance – standards are a way of regulating at a distance – but without problematizing different types of distance or how distance arises or how it is bridged (see Brunsson and Jacobsson 2000 or Timmermans and Epstein 2010). The research on standards and certification has above all discussed environment rather than distance. But environment and distance are connected since it is through the creation and perception of distance that the environment is formed. With this view of distance, it is not always clear what is within or outside of an organization, in the environment. Standards can enable the different units of a company to form a chain that geographically covers half of the globe. The units are then geographically distant from each other, but within the same organization and therefore not in 'the environment.' Here again, the drawing of a boundary between the organization and its so-called 'environment' become relative and fluid.

CONTROL AT A DISTANCE

When earlier researchers have stressed the global and international aspects of standards and certification, an implicit assumption has been that global or international control requires techniques other than those required to control locally or in close proximity. Standards and certification make it possible to control organizations in cases where the controlling entity and the entity controlled have no direct contact with each other.

Employing a view of distance (and globalization) other than absolute distance gives the concept of control at a distance a different meaning than when the controller and the controlled are able to have direct contact with each other: to see, hear and talk to each other.

One concept used to understand control at a distance is 'technologies of government' (Rose and Miller 1992), a development of Foucault's (1975/1987) theory on discursive power and discipline, that is, that people are disciplined to behave in a certain way without explicit or hierarchical monitoring to ensure that they actually do. People can be controlled at a distance, without direct monitoring, through 'self-control.' Higgins and Tamm Hallström (2007) interpret the emergence of standards based on ideas of discursive power and the technologies that uphold and enable this type of power. Standards' penetration in society has allowed them to infiltrate both the public and private sectors and constitute the basis for discursive control at a distance – standards represent an example of technologies of government (Higgins and Tamm Hallström 2007).

Other researchers (Law 1986; Latour 1987; Robson 1992; Sundström 2011; Corvellec, Ek, Zapata and Zapata Campos 2016) have discussed control at a distance using the concepts of inscriptions and artefacts. Inscriptions can be written texts, pictures, labels and numbers, and are a form of artefact – an object that makes organizing possible (Latour 1987). Artefacts enable control at a distance in that they can be moved from one place to another, from organization to organization. Following Law and Hetherington's reasoning (which builds in part on Law's earlier work from 1986) on distance as an effect of the assembling of people, objects (such as texts), time and relations, both control and distance become concepts with multiple dimensions. Distance is not a pre-existing given, but control and distance emerge together, in combination. This is a different interpretation of control at a distance than Foucault's and later Rose and Miller's analysis of discursive power. Using this interpretation, distance is not something to be covered or bridged by power or technologies. Distance is created with the same people, objects, time and relations that are to operate across that same distance (Corvellec, Ek, Zapata and Zapata Campos 2016).

Inscriptions are thus instruments for controlling at a distance. Inscriptions have two qualities that make control at a distance possible: they are mobile, and they are immutable (Latour 1987; Robson 1992). The mobility of inscriptions has to do with the requirement that they must be able to be physically moved in order to create action at a distance. The inscriptions also have to be movable over distances without changing, that is, they must be immutable or stable. Stability refers here to the inscriptions remaining unchanged and recognizable after having been moved. This has to do with 'the stability of relation between the inscription and the context to which it refers' (Robson 1992: 695).

Standards can be interpreted as a kind of inscription and thereby an instrument of control from a distance. Standards (which are written texts in a document) are mobile and can be moved from the standard-setting body to a dry cleaner in Kiruna, a Volvo plant in China, or an Indian restaurant in Nairobi. In order to control at a distance, the content of the standard must also be immutable, that is, it must remain the same no matter where the standard is used, and certification must mean the same thing no matter where the actual certificate is located.

In order to attain such stability of the inscription, an instruction, explanation or manual is needed, describing how the inscription is to work as a control instrument:

> At a more general level stability refers to the rules or rather conventions that relate a mobile inscription to its context. Thus, in cartography there are rules and conventions followed in the production of a map: specification of scale, of projection, and of perspective that allows such maps to be recognisable in relation to the area they depict. (Robson 1992: 695)

In other words, the control instrument needs an explanation or manual so that it can work in different locations, but in the same way.

Different inscriptions have different capacities to control at a distance. Robson (1992) describes how certain inscriptions have varying capacities to control at a distance, or in many contexts or situations at the same time. It is then not just a matter of the inscription bridging a physical distance, that is, moving something (a written text) from one place to another, but a matter of using that text to affect many situations or places at the same time: 'Action at a distance implies not merely physical space between two points, but the capacity, through "strong" explanations, to influence many contexts at the same time' (Robson 1992: 691). A standard might be an example of precisely such a 'strong explanation,' if it is accepted and thereby able to control others in many places at the same time.

If inscriptions in the form of texts are instruments for enabling control at a distance, how then, does that control work? Law described a technology enabling control at a distance, using the concepts of artefacts and inscriptions as instruments of control (in his study, he inspired both Latour (1987) and Robson (1992)). Law (1986) posed the question of how Portuguese ships that sailed to the other side of the world could be controlled from Lisbon back in the fifteenth century. His answer was that the Portuguese had powerful ships that they continually adapted to new waters, at the same time as they developed ways of translating astrological knowledge that crews could use to navigate. The documentation of how that navigation worked and how maps were to be read is an example of a manual or set of instructions for the control instrument – the maps. As written texts, the maps and manuals were also examples of inscriptions, texts that could be moved from Portugal and out to sea.

Law's model for control at a distance describes inscriptions as a kind of emissary – sent out to bridge distances. The point Law made is that texts (inscriptions), in combination with people and objects of different types, created a model for control at a distance. He summarized:

> Texts of all sorts, machines or other physical objects, and people, sometimes separately but more frequently in combination, these seem to be the obvious raw materials for the actor who seeks to control others at a distance. (Law 1986: 255)

A text alone does not create control. According to Law, a model for control at a distance builds on three components: texts, people and objects. In order to understand how control at a distance is made possible, it is crucial to know how the components relate to one another, how they are *juxtaposed* (Law 1986; Law and Singleton 2005). Juxtaposition represents something different from position or relation – juxtaposition refers to how a particular combination of components creates something, in that particular combination, that the components would not have been able to create on their own. Otherwise, a text is merely a text, a standard merely a standard, and an object merely an object. Robson (1992) describes this in terms of 'combinability,' that is, relating inscriptions to a context or to other inscriptions. Law (1986) discusses this in terms of structured elements: emissaries juxtaposed such that they together create a structure for control.

For the control to bridge distances, the juxtapositions of the components must create something lasting and powerful (Law 1986). According to Law, the capacity to do this is created by successively building the surrounding environment *into* the control rather than seeing the environment as a threat. By using various aids such as navigation tools and maps, the Portuguese sailors were able to control a hitherto unknown environment and thereby make it a part of their control (Law 1986). A control regime that incorporates the environment rather than being threatened by it becomes independent of its environment and thereby strong and resilient – the Portuguese ships were able to navigate new waters (the environment) by creating new navigation technologies and stronger ships. This enabled them to travel further and become a stronger fleet.

According to Law's idea, control at a distance would also need a capacity for communication that could not be distorted or interrupted. This is created via clear connections between the center and the periphery – 'no noise must be introduced into the circuit' (Law 1986: 241). In other words, to make control possible, the components of the control regime must be in contact with each other and maintain an unbroken communication. This unbroken communication link must in turn create the 'durable' and powerful nature that Law stresses is essential for control at a distance.

THE CONTROL REGIME – AN ANALYTICAL MODEL

The above reasoning sets the frame for how to understand organizing (organizing can occur within, among and outside organizations) and distance (distance can be cognitive, relational, spatial, temporal and geometric). I have at the same time presented how the organizing of and among organizations can be understood based on different organizing principles, as well as how organizations can be viewed as objects and thereby tools and components of a control regime. I have also presented techniques for how control at a distance is made possible. All in all, this makes up a model from which I can analyse the global control regime and its workings. The model builds on the three parts established above and that I expand upon here below.

Components in the Control Regime

The analytical model builds on the assumption that the control regime is made up of four different components: (1) a body that creates control instruments, (2) control instruments and manuals for the control instruments, (3) tools used to control, and (4) objects that are controlled.

The first component is the body that creates the control instruments used – these instruments do not just emerge on their own. Someone must write the texts used to control in the control regime.

The control instruments and manuals for the control instruments make up the second component. In Law's model (1986) and in following with Latour's concept (1987), control instruments are mobile and stable ('immutable mobiles'). In order to maintain this stability and mobility, a manual that explains how the instruments are to be used is required.

The third component is the tools used to control in the control regime. Tools can be different forms of control such as certification or accreditation. Tools can also be different organizations. Organizations are tools when they are used to exercise control.

To clarify, I call the components 'instruments' here when referring to inscriptions of different types, mainly standards but also the manuals that come with standards. When the components are organizations or other forms of control such as certification and accreditation, I call them 'tools.' The organizations and forms of control are used as tools to ensure that the control instruments are followed. The distinction between *instruments* and *tools* is drawn from Law's idea of three types of raw materials. Using my interpretation, standards correspond to texts, while organizations and forms of control correspond to tools.

The fourth component of the control regime is the object to be controlled. In Law's (1986) description, the objects to be controlled were ships that sailed from Portugal to other parts of the world, along with navigation and manuals for how the ships should be controlled, and trained seamen. In my analytical model, organizations are the objects to be controlled. In the analytical model, instruments (standards and manuals) and tools (organizations and the control forms of certification and accreditation) are used together to control objects (organizations). In other words, organizations can be both tools for controlling and objects that are controlled. The fact that organizations can be both control tools and controlled objects is fundamental for the construction of the control regime, and something that I will return to later in the analysis.

Juxtaposition of the Components

Earlier in the chapter I discussed the relevance of how the global control regime's components stand in relation to one another. In doing so I used the concept of juxtaposition to describe the components' relation or positioning to each other – certification means something when placed in relation to standards, accreditation means something when placed in relation to certification, and so on. How the components are juxtaposed is crucial for the global control regime's capacity to control. In order to create a durable and strong control regime, standards, certification and accreditation need to be combined with each other in different ways. The juxtaposition of components is an empirical matter, and it is these juxtapositions I will be looking for in my field data.

Controlling at a Distance Using Organizing Principles

At the beginning of the chapter, I presented a number of organizing principles, for example, the division of labor, coordination, standardization, formalization and hierarchy, which were initially presented as administrative principles or principles of bureaucracy but which, in the literature, have come to be reserved for the formal organization. Based on my interpretation of the literature, such principles can also be used to understand the organizing of and among organizations. In the field data I am about to present, I am looking for the following principles:

- Responsibility
- Division of labor
- Specialization
- Hierarchical authority
- Centralization
- Coherence
- Impartiality
- Coordination
- Rational authority
- Rules for procedures and processes
- Documented processes
- Formalization
- Standardization

If the construction of the control regime is to be understood as organizing of and among organizations, I should be able to find these principles of organizing in the global control regime. In other words, because, according to the analytical model, organizations are components of the regime, I make the assumption that the components are juxtaposed according to some or all of these principles.

THE ANALYTICAL MODEL

To summarize, I assume that the control regime is built with four components:

- a body that creates control instruments
- control instruments and manuals
- tools to control with (organizations and the control forms of certification and accreditation)
- objects to control (organizations)

The model builds on theoretical assumptions of how organizations, organizing and distance can be understood. Now, it is time to encounter the actual control regime. It did not start out as global, but as something national and in that sense local.

4. The Global Approach

This chapter starts with a description of what sort of order existed before the control regime was developed. The case of Sweden illustrates how a national state-run system for control and testing was exchanged for the private-law and global order that the control regime is. After that, I present the EC's (now the EU) attempts to create a common market free from technical trade barriers. To do this, the EC launched the *New Approach*. The aim of the New Approach was to regulate product characteristics and placed great importance on standards. To complement the New Approach, a system for controlling compliance with standards was later introduced – the *Global Approach.*

AN EXAMPLE OF A NATIONAL SYSTEM FOR CONTROL AND TESTING

Although ubiquitous in almost all aspects of today's life, the global control regime has not always existed. It has grown, step by step, over time. The story of Sweden might represent a case in point. Sweden went from a national and state-run testing system in the 1970s, to gradually incorporate the tools of the control regime, ending up in a completely global system.

In 1972, the Swedish government decided to make a holistic reform of testing activities nationwide. The National Testing System was created; seven national testing sites with monopoly over each respective testing area. This system was entirely state run: the rules for what should be tested, and how the testing should be conducted, were all issued by public authorities. Also, the testing was done on *physical* products *before* they were placed on the market. The arguments put forward for this particular system were that the state was the only actor in society independent enough from commercial interests to safeguard citizens from hazardous products. It was an all national, all public system where impartiality, objectivity and safety for society were key words.

However, the state-run national testing system was soon paralleled by a system based on private law. In the mid-1980s, initiatives were taken to change and improve the organizing of the then-10-year-old testing and control system. These change initiatives were linked to the 1980s' view of organizing of the public sector and the administrative policy trends that prevailed at that time. Most importantly, arguments about public safety and impartial state control were now exchanged for arguments about adapting Sweden to an international environment. In 1989 the Swedish government opened the floor to discussions of a more 'flexible' system. The international operations taking place under the General Agreement on Tariffs and Trade (GATT) and the European Free Trade Association (EFTA) were on the agenda, and control and testing were now placed in the context of international trade barriers.

In 1989 a governmental investigation was launched to map out the role of standardization in the EC/EFTA work (i.e. to investigate the role of the state in the development of standardization). The investigation is the first presentation of the control instrument of standards, which would come to have increasing importance in the emerging control regime. The aim of standardizing was to make things simpler by developing a consistent terminology, coordinating measurements and dimensions, specifying functions and characteristics. Standards were, in addition, to be factual and objective, and based on science. The starting point for the investigation was that standards have an increasing impact on areas that fall under the responsibility of the state. Thus, the state should direct its interest toward standardization.

The public investigation stressed that standards were private-law rules, at the same time as it pointed out that government authorities would need to participate in standardization contexts and use the results of standardization in its own regulations. The Swedish government predicted (rightly so) that an increasing amount of the authorities' work would have to do with standardization.

Even if authority representatives were involved in the development of a standard, through participating in various standardization meetings, it was emphasized that the division between public law on the one hand and standards as private rules on the other should be kept intact – a separation that would later fade when standards became control instruments and government regulations became manuals for those control instruments.

After introducing the most essential instrument in the regime (standards), two additional tools were introduced in the late 1980s: *self-monitoring* through *quality assurance*. These tools would gain increasing importance and come to form the foundation for still more tools: certification and accreditation. Here, the first orientation from the physical product toward the controlling of organizational routines was put forward. In quality assurance work carried out according to standards, the manufacturer documents its procedures for manufacturing routines and processes. The control is made of those routines, and not of the physical product.

Introducing self-monitoring was a new concept in public-law testing and control. Control was no longer being discussed in connection with the protection of lives, health and property, but with reducing control conducted by the state, by giving the manufacturer responsibility for carrying out controls on its own production.

In the early years of the control regime when the new tools were introduced, clear definitions of the various tools were still lacking. For example, certification could be a mandatory public-law control performed by an authority and certification thereby became an exercise by the state. Certification could also be carried out by separate, for-profit organizations. No clear boundary was drawn between private-law and public-law certification. Accreditation was presented in conjunction with mutual acceptance and international trade, but the difference between certification and accreditation was unclear: 'if the certification body is a laboratory, that performs both testing and certification, an accreditation of it is synonymous with a system certification of the laboratory' (SOU 1989:45: 10). However, in an attempt to become more clearly depicted in relation to other monitoring organizations, in 1990, the public authority for metrology and testing council, MPR, underwent a name change to become the board for technical accreditation, and was reborn under a more internationally viable name: *Swedac*. *Swedac* is still the name of the Swedish accreditation organization.

Step by step, the national testing system was now starting to be replaced by an emerging private law control regime. As a first step, the government allowed official testing and control to occur outside the National Testing System, at authorized testing sites. The government had now opened the way to more rules and more forms of control – a new control instrument and several new tools were presented in the form of standards, self-monitoring, certification and accreditation. For a period of time, the national public law system existed in parallel with the emerging standards-based control regime.

At the same time in Europe, the internal market of what was to become the European Union was emerging, and mutual acceptance was emphasized as a key concept. The free circulation of goods required that testing and control of products did not need to be repeated in every new country where the products were to be sold. Discussions of the mutual acceptance of testing and controls between countries drew attention to the value of trust in the control system. It was becoming harder and harder to keep the national all state-run testing system intact and in the late 1980s the use of official approvals as a form of verification began to be talked about not as public safety measures but as a barrier to trade. Standards were now unanimously seen as a better and more internationally viable instrument for regulating.

In 1991, the National Testing System was finally shut down and replaced by standards, certification and accreditation. The decommissioning of the national testing sites occurred without extensive political debate, to which Swedac's former director-general comments: 'I think I carried out the biggest de-monopolization of the 1990s, but we never talked about it' (Interview 8). This is symptomatic for the global control regime: it brings changes with huge societal impacts, but these changes are carried out in silence, under the radar.

In the following, I will describe what was put in place instead of national testing systems – the first steps taken in constructing the global control regime.

THE NEW APPROACH

The EC launched the idea of the 'internal market' based on an idea of a borderless market where goods, services and capital could flow freely between the member states (Council Resolution 85/C 136/01). Under regulation by detailed national rules, products were subject to different requirements in different countries – something that was seen as a technical barrier to trade and thereby a barrier to the internal market. The New Approach would harmonize product requirements between the countries by 'clear and coherent rules regarding product requirements and conformity assessment' (Prop. 1993/94:161: 4). In 1985, the Council of the Ministers of the EC presented the resolution that lay the foundations for the New Approach. Summarized, the four main principles were:

- Legislative harmonization is limited to the adoption (…) of the essential safety requirements (or other requirements in the general interest) with which products put on the market must conform, and which should therefore enjoy free movement throughout the Community.
- The task of drawing up the technical specifications needed for the production and placing on the market of products conforming to the essential requirements established by the Directives, while taking into account the current stage of technology, is entrusted to organizations competent in the standardization area.
- These technical specifications are not mandatory and maintain their status of voluntary standards.
- But at the same time national authorities are obliged to recognize that products manufactured in conformity with harmonized standards (...) are presumed to conform to the 'essential requirements' established by the Directive. (Council Resolution 85/C 136/01, Annex II)

The legislation of individual member states and the EC directive were to dictate only the most essential safety requirements, with the more detailed requirements to be found in standards. Standards and directives were linked to each other: if a manufacturer followed a specific standard noted in a directive, that manufacturer was presumed to satisfy the provisions of the directive. Standards would continue to be voluntary, but manufacturers could meet the mandatory requirements of a directive in other ways than following a standard as long as they were able to show how they met those requirements. The burden of proof was put with the manufacturer. Because the 'essential requirements' harmonize the legislation, this would enable products to be interchangeable across borders.

The New Approach also came with new forms of product directives, in which the most basic safety requirements were stated. The directives regulated different product categories: children's toys, pressure vessels, and so on. Each of the New Approach directives was linked to a standard. The standards regulated different risk categories, such as flammability, chemicals, and so on. The European Commission tasked the standardization bodies with issuing standards that matched the directives. Once a standard was published in the EC's official journal the standard became harmonized. Publication gave the standards legal effect (98/34/EC).

The New Approach increased the importance of standards, as noted here by the Swedish government in a government bill from 1992:

> Through EC's program for the internal market, standardization has been given a new and substantially more extensive role than it had before. It has become a tool for reducing technical barriers to trade and thereby for facilitating free trade. Standards will replace parts of regulation, for example, through authority regulations. (Prop. 1991/92:170 Annex 11: 5)

The principle of presumption (i.e. where conformity with a mandatory directive is presumed if a manufacturer is in compliance with a voluntary standard linked to that directive) had now become *the* principle to be followed in the product areas that fell under the New Approach. The 1985 Council of Ministers resolution also argued that, compared to national legislation, standards were a much more flexible way to regulate and, given that flexibility, should be used more.

To further strengthen the principles of the New Approach, a new system was created, where member states had to 'notify' the Commission of nationally issued technical regulations in the product areas covered by the New Approach (98/34/EC: 37).

The EU directive also stipulated the formation of a standing committee that would decide what should be regulated by standards under the New Approach and what could be regulated through national regulations. The committee (Committee on Standards and Technical Regulations), which came to be called the '98/34 Committee,' made up of delegates from the member states, also handled formal objections lodged against the standards published.

It was not only products that were regulated with the aid of standards. In step with the establishment of the New Approach, it was also advocated that the different forms of control in the EC were to be regulated. Certification, accreditation and manufacturer-conducted self-monitoring were all to be performed using standards as a reference. In other words, standards were used to regulate products (product standards) in the market, at the same time as standards were used to regulate the control of standard compliance (standards for forms of control). The principle of presumption came to apply to both requirements for products and control. If an accreditation body met the requirements laid out in the EN 45000 series of standards (for accreditation), it was presumed also to be competent with respect to the requirements of accreditation regulations and directives (Council Resolution 85/C 136/01).

In one interview I made during field work, standards are referred to as the skeletal structure of the New Approach (Interview 3), while in several others (Interviews 3, 20 and 19) it is pointed out that, even if standards do make up the skeleton or underlying foundation, and even if standards organizations, from a purely formal standpoint, own the standards, standards organizations are not responsible for how the standards are used or for what appears (or does not appear) in the standards. The interviewees note that it is the Commission that tasks the standards organizations with producing standards, and that it is ultimately the Commission that decides which standards are to be published, not the standards organizations. Standards organizations were gaining more and more impact, but relatively less responsibility.

THE GLOBAL APPROACH

When the EC launched the New Approach in 1985 an infrastructure to control compliance with the standards was also sought. In 1989, the Commission presented a proposal of such an infrastructure – the Global Approach (COM (89) 209 final – SYN 208). It was clear from the beginning that this set of tools was to be managed by the private sector and not public administrations in the member countries. Other defining points of the proposal were that the European structure was to be flexible and non-bureaucratic:

> In line with the separation of responsibilities between the private and public sectors required by the New Approach, this task should be assigned to the private sector rather than to the public authorities. Political control of the national and Community authorities must not be affected. (COM (89) 209 final – SYN 208: 25)

Translating these ideas into practice was not easy. In one interview it was expressed like this:

> ... There were a lot of years of uncertainty, and there was a big battle between national interests and the Commission on the other side. Because, if there was going to be an internal market, then you couldn't have every country's national testing body ruling on whether a product was approved. There had to be a uniform system for everyone and the EU didn't reign over the national bureaucracies. (Interview 8)

There are three recurring concepts in the proposal from 1989: the Global Approach must be transparent, it must be coherent, and it must instil confidence in certification, standards and accreditation. The Commission would therefore now establish a connection between certification, manufacturer-conducted self-monitoring and accreditation.

Confidence was presented as the first and foremost important argument: 'The necessity for a global approach to certification, inspection and testing thus arises out of this basic need to create conditions that are conducive to confidence' (COM (89) 209 final – SYN 208: 5). The concept of *confidence* appears throughout the entire communication, constituting the very basis for why the Global Approach was needed. The various arguments in the text then reinforce one another: confidence is achieved through *transparency*, transparency is achieved through coherency in how the Global Approach is designed, and coherency in turn creates confidence.

Interviewed employees at a certification company use the concept of *credibility* to highlight confidence as the basis for what they do: 'we gain credibility in that we are accredited in the same way as our customers [certified companies] gain credibility if they have a certificate' (Interview 5). During the interview, as in the proposal document, the importance of coherence is emphasized, that: 'everyone speaks the same language so that everyone understands each other, that there's a framework. That's the whole idea' (Interview 5).

CONFIDENCE AND ACCREDITATION

With the Global Approach, member countries were encouraged to create accreditation systems based on standards. This was a way of creating coherence between the different countries in the union. Accreditation was advocated as the method of priority for verifying the competence of certification companies.

Even though all of the EC countries were encouraged to establish systems for accreditation, the idea of creating a common accreditation organization was rejected:

> In view of the proposals concerning an overall European infrastructure for testing and certification ... the Commission does not feel that it is appropriate to encourage the setting up of a Community accreditation body which would unnecessarily lengthen the chain of responsibility and add unnecessary administrative and bureaucratic burdens without providing additional confidence. (COM (89) 209 final – SYN 208: 19)

Rather, the Commission wanted to create 'a network of the national networks' (COM (89) 209 final – SYN 208: 19). Just as before, during the reform of the national testing sites, the EC wanted to avoid unnecessary bureaucracy.

But industry did not see the emphasis on accreditation as a form of control as a good thing: 'as for accreditation, many people in industry were afraid that this would create another layer of bureaucracy on top of everything else' (Interview 8).

CONFORMITY ASSESSMENT

Despite a fear that the Global Approach would create new bureaucratic layers of control, the purpose of the Global Approach was to create a simpler, more flexible way of regulating and controlling the internal market. One way of doing this was to view testing and control as more than just technical tools. It was stressed that the Global Approach would not be limited to technical specifications for products. It was no longer limited to performing technical tests and testing physical products, but included also conducting controls of manufacturers' internal structures, for example, quality assurance systems for the production process (COM (89) 209 final – SYN 208: 18). The Global Approach was to be a system for assessing conformity, a concept that was considered more inclusive (COM (89) 209 final – SYN 208), covering quality systems, certification, testing and calibration.

What is not mentioned in the Commission's communication, however, is whether or not accreditation constitutes conformity assessment. The aim of accreditation was for it be something else, something over and above the other forms of control: 'the role of the accreditation body is for it to go a little further, for it to be the last control station' (Interview 4).

The Commission's communication regarding the Global Approach was followed by a resolution (90/C 10/01), thereby becoming formally decided. The importance of avoiding excessive bureaucracy in the organization for conformity assessment and mutual acceptance of controls between countries was stressed in the resolution as well (Council Resolution 90/C 10/01: 2).

THE PRINCIPLES OF THE GLOBAL APPROACH

So what is the Global Approach? It is a sort of framework based on interconnected principles for control and regulation. Modules for conformity assessment, manufacturer responsibility, notified bodies, the CE mark, and market surveillance.

The Modules for Conformity Assessment Procedures

In order to attain coherence in the increasingly divergent system of many different forms of conformity assessment, as a part of the Global Approach the

EC presented the 'modular approach' (COM (89) 209 final – SYN 208).[1] An early version of these modules is illustrated in Figure A.1, in the Appendix.

When it comes to control, the modules differ in their comprehensiveness on a rising scale from A to H. Module A is a declaration of conformity by the manufacturer in the form of written technical documentation. Module H is a declaration, in addition to the manufacturer's self-monitoring, that the manufacturer's quality system has also been controlled by a notified body. Modules B to G deal with type-controls and control of individual products to quality assurance of the manufacturer's production system.

The modules were aimed at both a product's design and construction phase and varied depending on the product's stage of development, the type of assessment to be carried out (documentation, type-control, quality assurance, inspection) and who was to perform the assessment (the manufacturer itself or a certification company), and could be combined in different ways depending on what was being manufactured: 'It is completely dependent on what kind of a product it is; the system is quite cleverly designed' (Interview 8).

Manufacturer Responsibility

Manufacturer responsibility was the second principle established in the Global Approach. Prior to the Global Approach, the manufacturer could be relieved of liability in cases where the requirements were set by public authorities. The introduction of the Global Approach confirmed that the responsibility lay with the manufacturer (Prop. 1993/94:161: 8) through self-monitoring, which was introduced in the New Approach.

The principle of manufacturer responsibility was a broadening of the principle of presumption: if a manufacturer did not follow a standard, either because there was no standard for a particular product or for other reasons, the manufacturer had to engage an independent external organization that could attest that the product complied with the requirements laid out in directives (COM (89) 209 final – SYN 208).

Regardless of whether a manufacturing process was to be controlled by a notified body or by controls carried out by the manufacturer itself, it would be the manufacturer who would bear the responsibility for the product.

The increased responsibility on the part of the manufacturer was motivated by the fact that manufacturers were assumed to want to maintain a good reputation, which would, the decision makers assumed, reduce the risk for cheating. Cheating carried the risk of undermining confidence in products, conformity assessment and, by extension, the entire internal market. But the manufacturer could make mistakes for other reasons, for example, by not knowing about a rule and therefore happening to break it:

> Sometimes if they [the manufacturers] do something wrong it might be that they just aren't aware of the legislation, because it's getting more and more complicated and *intertwined*. So it's sometimes really hard to keep track of which laws apply and there's a risk that the law is so complicated that it's difficult to understand. And that doesn't just apply to the manufacturers, but to the authorities too. (Interview 4)

This was confirmed in another interview, where the interviewee noted that most mistakes made by manufacturers are 'formal and administrative, that they make mistakes in the documentation itself' (Interview 19). In other words, by means of simplifying the system, it was becoming too complicated to handle for the involved parties.

Notified Bodies

A third principle of the Global Approach was that every assessment body, public or private, should be able to compete for assignments of performing conformity assessments (SOU 2006:113). In order to do this, official notification of the company or authority as a competent body must be made to the Commission, which was to be done by the member states. The names of notified bodies were published by the Commission in the *Official Journal of the European Communities* (OJ, now the *Official Journal of the European Union*). These bodies, usually certification companies, were notified as competent to control manufacturers in accordance with one New Approach directive at a time. That is, an assessment body could be notified several times, for different directives.

In Sweden, the task of attesting the competence of a body and notifying the Commission went to Swedac, the Swedish accreditation organization. There was a connection between this notification as a declaration of competence and accreditation as a declaration of competence, which motivated Swedac's being assigned to perform notifications to the Commission. A body accredited according to the EN 45000 series was also considered to meet the requirements of a notified body, hence a principle of presumption was thus created here as well.

The notification of bodies was a technical procedure outside the sphere of authorities. The notified bodies were not given the ability to decide on sanctions (coercive measures). On one hand, it is clearly stated several times in a government bill from 1994 that the notified bodies did not work on the mandate of the state and that their activities did not result in approval by an authority. On the other hand, however, this did not mean that government authorities could not operate as commercial control bodies. The underlying idea was for there to be competition between the bodies that performed conformity assessments (SOU 2006:113): all of the bodies judged to be competent could conduct conformity assessments.

The Global Approach did not state whether public authorities could participate in competition with other controlling organizations. However, the Swedish accreditation organization and the government agreed on that commercial control activities were argued not to be a public task, especially when they were not founded on political decisions and run under competitive conditions. This reasoning was well in line with the ongoing discussion of administrative policy at the time. A 1998 government bill on administrative policy (Prop. 1997/98:136) uses terms like 'refinement' and 'efficiency'.

The CE Mark

A fourth principle of the Global Approach was that it was given its own verification mark. Products that had undergone testing and control by either the manufacturer itself or by a notified body were to be labeled with the CE mark. Only the manufacturer could mark the product with the CE mark. In cases where a notified body had been involved in the process to assess conformity with a directive, the notified body's ID number was to appear next to the mark. Only one such mark indicating the product's compliance with the requirements of directives was permitted, while voluntary marks could be used to indicate that a product was in compliance with standards. The CE mark takes the form of a *C* and an *E* and stands for *Conformité Européenne*, the French for 'European Conformity' (see Figure 4.1).

The CE symbol was not to be understood as a mark that indicated safety or quality, but merely a verification by the manufacturer that the product meets the requirements laid out in directives:

> The CE mark has no other meaning than, if you, the manufacturer, place the CE mark on a product, you declare that it complies with the basic requirements of the directives, and it's not a brand. It was never intended to be, but sometimes it's been called that by journalists. (Interview 8)

And it is possible that the journalists were not alone in that misinterpretation:

> Somehow we always assume that the authorities have something to do with it. Many people believe that it's still an *ex ante* control procedure, that the CE mark is like the old S mark that stood for Swedish control or Swedish quality or Swedish testing and was a government mark, that is, an *ex ante* control by an authority that had approved a product to be released to the market. The S mark still exists, but it's a private control body, state-owned or half-state-owned, that owns the mark. (Interview 4)

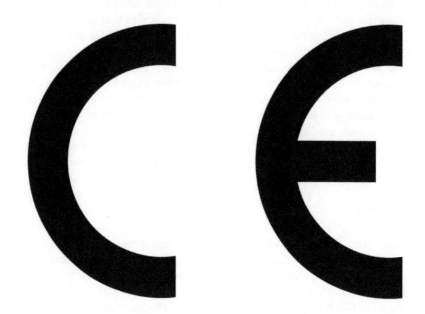

*Figure 4.1   An early version of the CE mark (A Global Approach to
                   Certification and Testing COM (89) 209 final – SYN 208: 23)*

To reduce confusion, only the manufacturer and no other organization should put the mark on the product. Around 1992, the EC had reached an agreement regarding the mark's appearance with respect to the size and proportions of the *C* and *E* lettering. For example, the mark could be no less than five millimetres in height.

The Swedish CE-marking act (SFS 1992:1534), states that the CE mark may only be placed on products that comply with EC directives or authority regulations. The CE mark must have set proportions, and must be clearly visible, legible, and durable. Anyone who places the CE mark on a product that does not meet directive requirements must pay a penalty. Thus it became against the law to not mark goods that should be marked, and against the law to mark goods that should not be marked.

Market Surveillance

A fifth principle of the Global Approach was that of the so called market surveillance. This is the control made of products after they have been put on the market, and constitutes the last step in the step-by-step idea of control, presented in the modules. It was up to each member country to organize its own market surveillance – the Global Approach and the 1989 resolution regulated only that there should be market surveillance, not how it should be organized. In Sweden, a government bill on market surveillance for product safety came in 1994 (Prop. 1993/94:161) and included guidelines for how market surveillance should be organized in Sweden. The definition given in the bill read: 'By "market surveillance" the EC is referring to an established form of control of product safety. This must be kept separate from the control that occurs within the framework of the stated procedures for assessment of conformity' (p. 7). Market surveillance is thus distinguished from other tools in the Global Approach.

The New Approach redrew the division of control in the life of a product. Self-conducted control by the manufacturer or control via a notified body was to replace *ex ante* state control by way of authority approval in the design and production phases. The market surveillance occurred after the product was placed on the market: 'Market surveillance is the last link in the chain of technical measures to prevent products that are substandard from a safety standpoint from being taken into use and causing accident and injury' (Prop. 1993/94:161: 22).

The purpose of market surveillance, as described by the government in the 1994 bill, was to maintain confidence in the internal market. As one inter-viewee put it, market surveillance is the system's 'sump pump, gathering up everything that slips through' (Interview 3).

Sector-by-Sector Oversight Responsibility

At the time the 1994 government bill was proposed, there was still no coherent or unified regulation for market surveillance in either the EC or Sweden.

The Swedish government decided to allow authorities to be responsible for market surveillance based on already-existing oversight responsibilities and regulatory areas, which would minimize changes to the authority structure. The bill therefore refers to this as a 'minimum solution.'

Two measures were needed to establish this minimum solution. One was clarification of the instructions in order to clarify the responsibility of the respective authorities. Several of the bodies consulted pointed out that this responsibility could be difficult to determine in that the EC's directives were drawn up in such a way that they did not necessarily line up with the bounda-ries drawn between Swedish authorities responsible for oversight: for example, a product could fall under the area of responsibility of both the Chemicals Agency and the National Electrical Safety Board. No definitive division of responsibility between the authorities was given in the government bill.

Because responsibility had been decentralized, an organization was needed to which companies and other stakeholders could turn to receive coordinated information on market surveillance. The second measure needed was thereby a coordinating organization to serve as a contact point. The idea of creating an entirely new authority tasked with coordinating market surveillance was rejected. Instead, discussion centered around which of the current authorities would be given the additional task of coordinating other market surveillance authorities, and the responsibility fell to Swedac, the Swedish accreditation organization. It was furthermore proposed that a council be created, where representatives from the responsible sectoral authorities could meet and confer.

One difference between regular state supervision and market surveillance is that market surveillance authorities use standards in their control. When asked what role standards play for the market surveillance authorities, one interviewee's answer was that: 'A huge role, most products are covered by standards because it's standards we use as the measuring stick' (Interview 19). Another interviewee stated that 'everything is so much easier if there's a standard, but we're not required to look at the standard,' because 'the use of standards is voluntary for the manufacturer' (Interview 25).

Ten years after the first government bill came a report on market surveillance. An investigative committee on supervision of product safety and open markets (SOU 2004:57) had been commissioned to – 'without preconceptions of the current organization' (Dir. 2003:34: 203) – come up with proposals on how Swedish market surveillance could be designed in order to enhance the market surveillance in both Sweden and the EU. The committee was further tasked with charting the need for market surveillance in different product areas, putting forward proposals for dividing the responsibility between market surveillance authorities, and coming up with a proposal for how market surveillance was to be financed.

The background to the investigation was the accelerated pace of product development, and the government therefore wanted a review of how the market surveillance was organized. The findings of the committee were that the political governance of market surveillance was 'too weak' and that there was 'little direction regarding how the authorities were to prioritize' (SOU 2004:54: 12).

The investigators were of the mind that it was not uncommon for uncertainties to arise regarding the authorities' areas of responsibility and that there was a great need for the state to gain an overview of the control and the division of labor in the field of market surveillance.

One of the measures proposed by the investigators to address the problem of an unclear division of responsibility was that a new regulation regarding market surveillance be created and that the political objective of governing market surveillance be clarified therein (SOU 2004:57).

In the investigation, the possibility was addressed once again of gathering market surveillance under a centralized authority, rather than the decentralized, sector-by-sector organization that currently existed: 'The problem with overlapping areas of responsibility, which is at present somewhat of a barrier for authorities and for manufacturers, should be able to be avoided. Having a single authority to which manufacturers and the public could address their questions and complaints would suffice' (SOU 2004:57: 147).

Nevertheless, the investigation's final proposal was to keep the decentralized sectoral order, and the committee's report formed the foundations of Proposition 2004/05:98, the ensuing government bill containing guidelines for market surveillance of products etc. In the bill, the government stressed that 'a more coherent and nation-wide market surveillance system should be sought' (Prop. 2004/05:98: 24). The bill essentially followed the report's proposal to keep the sector-by-sector organizing with responsibility divided between the supervisory authorities. Given the continuation of this system, the government also proposed that the management of market surveillance authorities be more explicit.

In keeping with the report, the government proposed that the coordinating and contact function remain with Swedac, but that the Market Surveillance Council should be given a clearer role. This included that the council would start to report annually on its work. In addition, it was proposed that two new authorities – Swedish Customs and the National Board of Trade – also join the Market Surveillance Council. The ensuing regulation issued in 2005 lists the authorities tasked with market surveillance and that thereby became a part of the Market Surveillance Council.[2]

OPEN SYSTEM FOR TESTING AND CONTROL

Following the decision regarding the introduction of the Global Approach in Sweden in 1991, no additional overarching decisions regarding the organization for testing and control were issued until 2006. Sweden's membership in the EU did not affect the organizing of control. The big change occurred in connection with Sweden joining the EEA. When it joined the EU, the organization for testing and control was already in place.

In 2006, an investigation into Sweden's open system for testing and control presented an evaluation of the 15 years the system had been in existence (SOU 2006:113). In the directives (Dir. 2005:138), the government had stated that no full investigation had been carried out since the Global Approach had been introduced. By 'open system' was meant a system open for different control organizations to perform conformity assessments in competition with one another.

The investigation discussed testing and control mainly with reference to effectiveness, competition, neutrality in competition, and cost efficiency – representing a change from the government bills of the 1970s in which the discussion concerned mainly safety, health and protection of lives and property. Those arguments were still present, but in the background: 'Society's endeavor is therefore to technical control orders that provide good protection but that are also cost-effective' (SOU 2006:113: 41).

The investigator was consistently in favor of the open system for testing and control, pointing out that during the 15 years that the system had existed much had happened with respect to globalization and the pace of product development. It was nevertheless stated that open systems appeared to be rational and effective, and that open systems could be assumed to be more transparent than non-open systems (SOU 2006:113).

The investigation furthermore submitted that the only thing needed for an open system to work is a requirements document, and that this requirements document be formulated so precisely that independent assessors following the same document would arrive at the same result. According to the investigation, the requirements must be verbalized, explained and documented, which was thought to be most easily accomplished through reference to a standard (SOU 2006:113).

The need for clear requirement specifications is stressed also in an interview with a certification company. One of the elements in how the open system becomes 'open', is that certification companies can take over each other's customers (e.g. manufacturing companies). With clear requirements, it should not really matter which certification firm takes control. Therefore, it became important that there be continuity in the interpretation of standards and other requirement documents. Such continuity in the work of certification companies would best be ensured through accreditation (Interview 5).

During this time period, attention was drawn to the global relevance of standards and the state administration's position on this in a 2007 communication from government (Skr. 2007/08:140). The communication encourages the Government Offices of Sweden to take a more active role in standardization work. The 2006 investigation and 2007 communication describe standards as flexible, rational and international regulating tools. When interviewed, the author of the communication described the work of informing Government Offices' officials of the importance of standards as 'pioneer work' and like clearing a path where no-one has gone before' (Interview 17).

ROLES STILL UNCLEAR

Even when accreditation and certification were first introduced in Sweden during the National Testing System era it was unclear when accreditation and certification should be used. This lack of clarity was cited later as well, in the evaluation from 2006 (SOU 2006:113): there did not appear to be any clear principles regarding when the competence of organizations was to be assessed through accreditation or through certification. There was no clear pattern of when one form of control should be chosen over another. The investigator did, however, state that the various forms of control involved a varying number of steps to the object being controlled: for example, compared with certifi- cation, accreditation was one step further away from the controlled object. Another perspective regarding the length and distance covered by the steps was highlighted in an interview where the distinction between accreditation and certification in terms of the varying number of steps to society or the market, but where accreditation, as a publicly performed task, lies closer to society than certification – and accreditation gone wrong can, according to the legislation on administrative procedure, be revoked (Interview 8), which certification cannot. Another interviewee describes accreditation as a 'formal test of competence' and – when asked if certification was not also a formal test of competence – describes certification as an 'attestation of conformity' adding that the fact that a product meets a specified requirement 'has nothing to do with competence' (Interview 3).

THE ACCREDITATION ORGANIZATION

The changes entailed with the Global Approach gave the Swedish accredi- tation organization Swedac an increasingly central role. First, accreditation was given a more coordinated and central role in the Global Approach. Accreditation was the control that was to be carried out to assess the compe- tence of other bodies that perform conformity assessments (COM (89) 209 final – SYN 208). In Sweden, Swedac was the body that did this accrediting, and the authority's role became even clearer when the government decided that only Swedac would perform accreditation (Prop. 2004/05:98).

The evaluation of the open system (SOU 2006:113) proposed, in addition, that it should be clarified in law that Swedac's exclusive right to perform accreditation applied not only to the harmonized area that fell under the New Approach, but also to the voluntary area: 'Such a change would help to clarify and increase the credibility of accreditation and the open system' (SOU 2006:113: 14).

Yet another measure that gave Swedac a central role was the government decision that the responsibility for appointing notified bodies would also be placed with Swedac. At an earlier stage, this had been the government's responsibility, but it was then transferred to Swedac. Decisions were also taken giving Swedac a coordinating role in market surveillance, whereby Swedac was called on to convene and chair the Market Surveillance Council (SOU

2004:57, Prop. 2004/05:98). Swedac was also assigned the task of listing all of the authorities that were part of the Market Surveillance Council and drawing up action plans for market surveillance. All of the authorities that set testing and control regulations were required to consult with Swedac first.

Several of the texts presented in and around the 2004–2006 period noted that a review of the Global Approach was being carried out in the EU. The process in the EU had begun in 2003 and would come to be called the 'Goods Package' and consist of three pieces of legislation. Together, these legal measures reinforce the organization established over the more than 25 years during which the Global Approach has emerged. In the next chapter, I present the Goods Package.

NOTES

1. A supplementary decision from 1993 (93/465/EEC) describes the modular approach in more detail.
2. These were: the Swedish Work Environment Authority, the National Board of Housing, Building and Planning, the National Electrical Safety Board, the Swedish Energy Agency, the Chemicals Agency, the Swedish Consumer Agency, the Medical Products Agency, the Swedish Environmental Protection Agency, the Swedish Post and Telecom Authority, the Swedish Press and Broadcasting Authority, the Swedish Civil Contingencies Agency, the National Board of Health and Welfare, the Swedish Tax Agency, Swedac, the Swedish Transport Agency, the National Board of Trade, and Swedish Customs. (SFS 2005:893 Regulation on Market Surveillance of Goods).

5. The Goods Package

In this chapter, I will paint the picture of a system that grows global, a system that, via the EU, branches out across the world. The historic account that started out in the Swedish National Testing System, and became nestled in the European structure, now forms the regime as we know it today. But many steps were taken in order to put the 'global' in the global control regime.

THE GOODS PACKAGE

In 2003, the EU initiated a review of the Global Approach and the New Approach. The review led to the so-called 'Goods Package of 2008,' consisting of three legislative acts: (1) Regulation 764/2008 on the application of certain national technical rules to products lawfully marketed in another member state, (2) Regulation 765/2008 on the requirements for accreditation and market surveillance, and (3) Decision No. 768/2008 on a common framework for marketing of products. The Goods Package was motivated as follows:

> It is very difficult to adopt Community legislation for every product which exists or which may be developed; there is a need for a broad-based legislative framework of a horizontal nature to deal with such products, to cover lacunae .... (765/2008/ EC: 30)

The 'lacunae' referred to in the cited passage are gaps or missing parts created by the New Approach and the Global Approach. With the introduction of the Goods Package, the system established in the EC in 1985 was given a legal foundation and now also a set of guidelines for how the legislative acts should be interpreted. The guiding documents are official and published by, among others, the Commission. The 'Blue Guide,' for example, on the implementation of product rules, provides descriptions of accreditation, conformity assessment, the modular system, market surveillance, CE marking, conformity assessment bodies and notified bodies, the principle of presumption, and the roles of the economic actors or 'operators.' As shown in this quote, the parts of the package are presented as interlinked:

> All these different elements are interlinked, operate together and are complementary, forming an EU quality chain. The quality of the product depends on the quality of the manufacturing, which in many instances is influenced by the quality

of testing, internal or carried out by external bodies, which depends on the quality of the conformity assessment processes, which depends on the quality of the bodies which in turn depends on the quality of their controls, which depends on the quality of notification or accreditation; the entire system depending on the quality of market surveillance .... If one element goes missing or is weak, the strength and effectiveness of the entire 'quality chain' is at stake. (Blue Guide, Version 1.1: 12).

A COMMON TERMINOLOGY AND A COMMON FRAMEWORK

Decision No. 768/2008/EC created the legislative framework for how the directives created within the New Approach should be composed. When new directives were drafted or older directives revised, they were to follow the framework laid out in this decision.

One of the frameworks clarified with the Goods Package was the modular system, presented in Chapter 4, that came into being in 1989. The point was made, for example, that the notified bodies should not increase the burden on the economic operators (i.e. the manufacturer, the importer, the distributor) that must be able to compete on a level playing field, regardless of which notified body they dealt with. Achieving such equal competitive conditions required that the notified bodies follow a coherent approach in their application of the modules, that they maintain the same technical level and be equally meticulous in their work, and that they set the same requirements. The controls performed by the notified bodies within the modular system were to be based on ISO 9000 quality system standards (Blue Guide, Version 1.1). The purpose of this was to not let the system 'grow wild,' as one interviewee noted (Interview 3).

Another way of creating such a tidy system and preventing wild growth was to introduce a common terminology. Both Decision 768/2008/EC and Regulation 765/2008/EC provided a list of definitions for the Goods Package's central concepts:

> In the past, legislation on the free movement of goods has used a set of terms partly without defining them and guidelines for explanation and interpretation have consequently been necessary. ... This Decision therefore introduces clear definitions of certain fundamental concepts. (768/2008/EC: 83)

The list provides definitions of the concepts contained in the Goods Package. Common definitions for *importers*, *distributers* and *technical specifications* were also needed. A number of these terms and definitions are described in more detail below.

Economic Operators

Decision No. 768/2008/EC clarified who the 'economic operators' were. A definition was already given in the list of definitions, but the articles of the regulations explained the various roles in even more detail. It was mainly the division of responsibility between the different actors that was defined, as well as their relation to each other.

The Manufacturer

Manufacturer responsibility was established during the 1980s when the EU replaced *ex ante* approval by an authority with self-conducted production controls by manufacturers themselves, but the Goods Package gave the manufacturer a clearer responsibility. Certain tasks were to be conducted only by the manufacturer: the manufacturer was the only economic operator that was to perform its own conformity assessment and draw up the manufacturer declaration. As I have shown above, the manufacturer was also the only one who could CE-mark the product: 768/2008/EC also decided that the manufacturer's name, the registered trade name or trademark, and an address where it can be contacted must appear on the product or, if this is not possible, on the product packaging or in a document that accompanies the product.

The Importer

The importer is the economic operator that brings a product not produced in the EU into the internal market. The reason for assigning responsibility to the importer as well (and not leave the manufacturer with all of the responsibility for the goods on the market), was that the EU needed a kind of border guard between the its internal market and those who manufacture products outside of the market, because a market surveillance authority 'can't take a Chinese company to Swedish court' (Interview 20). It would be the importer that placed the product on the internal market (768/2008/EC) and that therefore would be responsible for ensuring that the product complies with the requirements of directives. The importer was not to perform conformity assessment itself, but was to make sure that the manufacturer had fulfilled its obligations. The importer's name, registered trade name or trademark, and contact address were also to appear on the product. Even though the EU wanted to create clearer roles for the economic operators, one interviewee pointed out that one problem with the new role for importers was that in e-trade contexts it is not always clear who has that role (Interview 26). Global trading and new patterns of consumption and production has the former physical and geographical borders blurred out.

The Distributer

The distributer is the economic operator that sells the products to the end customer. Sometimes, the manufacturer and the distributor is the same organization, and in some circumstances the obligations of economic operators could change. Importers and distributers could be assigned the manufacturer's obligations in cases where they modified the product in some way, such as changing the name of the product, importing or selling the product under their own name (and not that of the manufacturer), or changing the color of the packaging, so that it would no longer be certain whether the product complied with the directive (768/2008/EC: 84). An example of how problematic this transfer of responsibility through the manufacturer's role could be was noted in two interviews. The example was a scenario in which a package of balloons is CE-marked, which clearly links the responsibility to the balloon manufacturer who affixed the CE mark to the package. But if that package is opened at a McDonald's restaurant, for example, and the balloons are blown up and given to children there – balloons that, individually, do not carry the CE mark – then who would have the responsibility for each single and separate balloon? (Interview 22 and Interview 25).

A Supply Chain

Decision No. 768/2008/EC also clarified the relationship of economic operators to one another by emphasizing that the operators were part of a supply chain. All economic operators were to know which other operators were involved in a product's specific supply chain. Clarification was given of the different tasks of the different operators in relation to each other when the operators were located in different places in the world in relation to each other and the EU's internal market.

Confusing to an outsider, the roles were not always clear even to the economic operators themselves, which the balloon example highlights. An interview with a trade association that represents various economic operators indicates that companies do not always know what their role is and that it has above all become more difficult for distributors to shoulder the increased responsibility assigned to them (Interview 24): the new division of roles 'has caused problems for a lot of operators' (Interview 20) who don't know that they are formally considered the manufacturer if they import a product under their own name. An interviewee from a product company describes how such divisions of responsibility have become increasingly complicated, that the company can be the manufacturer, the importer and the distributor – all at the same time (Interview 22).

The EC guides were published to help distinguish the roles of economic operators, but Swedish market surveillance authorities also provided help.

CE MARKING AND GREY ZONES

The Goods Package also included clear directives for the handling of CE marking. Regulation 765/2008/EC states that 'the CE marking, indicating the conformity of a product, is the visible consequence of a whole process comprising conformity assessment in a broad sense' (765/2008/EC: 33). The Goods Package also made the link between CE-marking and the manufacturer more explicit – as noted, the manufacturer was the only one who could CE-mark a product.

Once again it was established that the CE mark would be the only marking used to indicate products' compliance with the requirements of the New Approach directives:

> The affixing to a product of markings, signs or inscriptions which are likely to mislead third parties regarding the meaning or form of the CE marking shall be prohibited. Any other marking may be affixed to the product provided that the visibility, legibility and meaning of the CE marking is not thereby impaired. (765/2008/EC: 43)

All products sold in the EU should not be marked, however – only products regulated under New Approach directives are to be CE-marked, no others. This led to confusion among manufacturers, who began to CE-mark their products just to be safe (Interview 4). One interviewee describes how the Commission undertook an information campaign encouraging consumers to 'look for the CE marking,' a campaign that was criticized for confusing consumers. For example, toys were to be CE-marked but closely related products such as pacifiers were not, making it difficult for the consumer to know whether they should look for the CE mark or not. The campaign led to manufacturers incorrectly 'forcing CE marking' (Interview 20).

That is, there could be for some a lack of clarity surrounding what type of product one sold, imported and/or manufactured. How the product was defined became important since this had consequences for whether it should be CE-marked or not. Terms such as 'grey zone products' suggested that it was not always obvious how certain products should be classified.

Defining one's product in relation to the market surveillance also became important for economic operators, because the market surveillance authorities could decide which authority would be responsible for supervision and this, in turn, was determined by how the product was defined. The problem of grey zones related in part to product classification and in part to the division of responsibility between supervisory authorities. In an interview with one market surveillance authority, this was expressed as follows:

> Which authority is responsible for what – that's a difficult question not only when it comes to product grey zones, but there's also a huge grey zone regarding … who should cover what. For instance, a bike trailer, that you attach to a bicycle, is an articulated vehicle and thus falls under the Transport Agency. But bike trailers can also be used to transport children, which does happen …. Then who's responsible for supervision? The Consumer Agency is responsible for prams and strollers so … quite often there are discussions like that. (Interview 25)

REGULATION OF NOTIFIED AS WELL AS NOTIFYING BODIES

Through the legislative acts of the Goods Package, the EU began to regulate not only the notified bodies and notification procedures, but also the notifying authorities. A more coherent system for both the notified and the notifying bodies was also one of the main purposes of the Goods Package (765/2008/ EC). The EU found it problematic that different countries used different procedures when it came to the notification process itself. The notifying bodies were now given a territorial basis:

> Each member country designates the notified bodies within its own territory. The manufacturer can go to the notified body in the territory where he has his operations, or to someone else, but the notified bodies in Sweden, they're appointed by Sweden; Sweden, the member state, appoints its own notified bodies, but once a notified body has become notified, then it can operate throughout the entire internal market, that's the point. But Sweden can't notify a body that's established in Denmark. To become a notified body in Sweden, you have to be a Swedish legal person and be established in Sweden. (Interview 18)

The legislative acts established that, if the notifying body was not a public authority, it must be a legal person.

The Goods Package also presented more and extended requirements on 'independence', now applicable to a larger set of organizations. Even other notifying bodies were required to be impartial and independent, requirements that until that point had applied to the notified bodies (which were certification companies). The notifying bodies had to be independent from the bodies being notified, that is, bodies that conducted assessments of conformity.

Regarding the bodies notified, that is, usually certification companies, the acts established that these bodies also had to be legal persons. For them, the requirements were clarified with respect to objectivity and their independence in relation to what the notified body controlled. This meant that employees of a certification company could not participate at all in the design, manufacturing, marketing, installation or use of the products being assessed. Neither could they use consultancy services for the companies they were to certify. This was considered potentially harmful to the certification company's independence, impartiality and integrity as the inspecting body (768/2008/EC, Art. R17).

MUTUAL RECOGNITION

All products found in the EU's internal market do not fall under the directives of the New Approach, and for the handling of products not regulated under harmonized areas in the EU, the EU presented Regulation 764/2008/EC. This regulation addresses the technical rules that are drawn up by the member countries but not harmonized, that is, that are not regulated by the EU but by the respective member countries. The idea was to open up the procedures for the authorities rule-setting to make them more accessible and simplify administrative procedures to make them less of an obstacle.

Regulation 764/2008/EC linked the principle of mutual recognition not only to recognition of products between countries, but also to conformity assessment (e.g. certification) and recognition of the level of competence of such assessments by way of accreditation. The countries in the EU were to accept the different forms of conformity assessment performed under accreditation, regardless of which EU country the accreditation was performed in.

ACCREDITATION'S ROLE CLARIFIED

One of the most important aspects of the Goods Package was the role given to accreditation. Accreditation was to assume an increasingly important function in the EU's organizing of the internal market.

Regulation 765/2008/EC presented accreditation in a context: 'Accreditation is part of an overall system, including conformity assessment and market surveillance, designed to assess and ensure conformity with the applicable requirements' (765/2008/EC: 31). But accreditation also received a very specific role in this context: 'The particular value of accreditation lies in the fact that it provides an authoritative statement of the technical competence of bodies whose task is to ensure conformity with the applicable requirements' (765/2008/EC: 31). Here again, it is clearly stated that accreditation is a control of the controls, the final step. The Goods Package was to:

> ... clarify that accreditation is the top level of the quality infrastructure and one way of doing that is to say that there has to be a legal body and it has to be an exercise of authority. The accreditation bodies may not compete with each other, they may not compete with the objects they supervise, may not perform any kind of conformity assessment, that which the certification body does. The accreditation body may not

do that, even if the assessment is very similar ... but it's the different levels that are important. (Interview 18)

Another interviewee describes accreditation as the best way to safeguard control of compliance: 'For new directives and for new regulations, if they want to have a process of ensuring that the regulation is carried out correctly, they should be calling up accreditation' (Interview 13).

One way to clarify the specific role of accreditation was precisely to separate accreditation from conformity assessment, for example, certification. That was done by clarifying that accreditation could only be carried out on organizations that work with conformity assessment, not the objects that could be certified, for example, physical products or people.

FOUR PRINCIPLES OF ACCREDITATION

The regulation clarifies the specific role of accreditation in four ways: (1) providing legally binding grounds for accreditation, (2) stipulating that each member state may appoint only one accreditation body – a national accreditation body (NAB), (3) stipulating that accreditation not be operated in competition with other accreditation bodies, and (4) that national accreditation bodies must be formally recognized as public authorities. (765/2008/EC).

Regulation 765/2008/EC also contains a specific article (Art. 6) prohibiting competition between national accreditation bodies with conformity assessment bodies or with other national accreditation bodies (765/2008/EC: 36). This would eliminate competition between accreditation bodies, and between accreditation bodies and certification companies. The idea of non-competition was a strong one, and was based on there being only one accreditation body per country, a point that was emphasized as important in the design of the Goods Package.

By introducing this regulation, the EU wanted to give all accreditation organizations the status of a public authority. In the case of Sweden, this did not mean any major changes since Swedac, the Swedish accreditation body, was already a public authority. In other cases, through special contracts with the government, the accreditation organizations were assigned the role of an official public authority, even those that were private companies. This was the case, for example, in the UK (Interviews 13 and 15).

The regulation also stipulated that the national accreditation bodies could not operate on a for-profit basis, which was connected in part to their status as a public authority, in part to the requirement that they be the last link of the quality chain, in part to the fact that they performed a 'task in the public interest' (Blue Guide, Version 1.1: 83), and in part to the fact that accreditation was not a commercial activity: 'If you've got different accreditation bodies operating in the same field, and they're private bodies that are commercial, then of course some of their decisions may be made on a commercial basis because they don't want to lose customers' (Interview 13).

Even though the Goods Package involved changes for the member countries' accreditation bodies, the new initiatives of the Goods Package generated little if any political debate: drafting of the regulation was 'very, very low key' because, accreditation activities were seen as 'a bit of a backwater' (Interview 15).

SWEDAC AND STANDARDS

The Goods Package stipulated that accreditation organizations should have special status in relation to other organizations in the quality infrastructure. The EU's decision now not only gave the Swedish accreditation organization Swedac a clear role in the EU, but also a clear role in Swedish state administration:

> Furthermore, the responsibilities and tasks of the national accreditation body have to be clearly distinguished from those of other national authorities. This provision aims to enhance the independence of the national accreditation body and the impartiality and objectivity of its activities. Should the national accreditation body be part of a larger public structure, such as a ministry, other departments are not allowed to influence accreditation decisions. (Blue Guide, 92)

The new law thereby formally designated Swedac as Sweden's national accreditation body, giving it the right also to decide on penalties to be paid by those who fraudulently claimed to be accredited but were not (SFS 2011:791 §23).

How the accreditation organizations should be organized in relation to one another was also set out in the Goods Package, though how these bodies should work was regulated by standards. It was now mainly ISO 17011 that guided the work of the accreditation organizations – a standard that targeted accreditation organizations. The Blue Guide defines accreditation by linking to standards: 'a process of transparent and impartial evaluation against internationally recognized standards' (Blue Guide, Version 1.1: 88). Standards were once again put forward as the very basis of the 'quality infrastructure' and the role of standards was further strengthened by the Goods Package. In addition, the use of standards was now linked not only to EU's internal market, but to international trade in general.

The increasingly explicit connection between accreditation and standards had an impact on Swedac, which thereby became to an increasing extent formally controlled by standards.

ISO 17011 fell under this principle of presumption. This meant that if the accreditation organizations were in compliance with the requirements of ISO 17011, they also met the requirements of the EU regulations. This in turn meant that, as a public authority, Swedac came to be controlled by ISO 17011. That a public authority was regulated by an international standard was described as something new: 'That had never been stated in law before, so explicitly. It's always been in Swedac's official appropriations and instructions from government that we have to work with or meet international standards, but not this explicitly ... it's never been regulated like that before' (Interview 18). Another interviewee described Swedac's relation to standards as: 'standards have a much greater effect on our activities than government or ministry regulations' (Interview 3).

The division or roles and control through standards is illustrated in Swedac's presentation material (Figure 5.1), which depicts the standard Swedac follows in its own work, with the standards Swedac works with when controlling other organizations' compliance with standards underneath. Thus Swedac used standards to control others and was itself controlled by a standard. Once again, the line between the controller and the controlled becomes increasingly blurred.

The result of accreditation can be seen in the form of an accreditation mark that carries the Swedac logo (see Figure 5.2).

Once a conformity assessment company has been accredited by Swedac, it can use the Swedac logo in its own certification or inspection activities. The certification company then places the logo on the certificate it issues to its customer, a production company, for example. The use of elements of the country's coat of arms in its logo is not unique to Swedac, but is something that has been used by most national accreditation bodies. In the UK, for example, where the accreditation body – UKAS – was not a public authority (UKAS is a company that was given the status of a public authority in accordance with the principles of accreditation described above), a licensing agreement was drafted to allow UKAS to use the royal crown in its logo (BIS 2011). That crowns are used in the logos is no coincidence: one interviewee noted that the customers of accreditation bodies (i.e. the certification companies) set a high value on the crowns, especially those who worked mainly at the national level (Interview 14). It was becoming more and more important to tie the accreditation organization to the idea of the nation state.

MARKET SURVEILLANCE DEFINED

In Regulation 765/2008/EC, the EU presented a common framework for market surveillance. The member states were to 'establish appropriate communication and coordination mechanisms between their market surveillance authorities'

SWEDAC

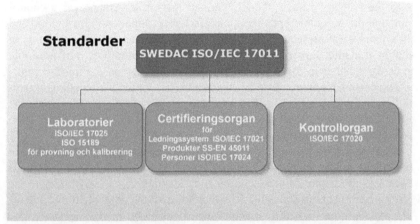

Note: The standards shown in the diagram were later updated, in September 2016. The dark grey bubble on top says Swedac 17011, the light grey bubbles to the left say: Laboratory ISO/IEC 17025 and ISO/IEC 15189 Testing and collaboration. Middle bubble says Certification bodies – ISO/17021, products SS-EN 45011, persons ISO/IEC 17024, and the bubble to the right reads Control bodies ISO/IEC 17020.
Source: Presentation material obtained during an interview.

Figure 5.1   Swedac and standards

Note: Swedac accreditation.
Source: www.swedac.se.

Figure 5.2   The Swedac logo

(765/2008/EC: 39). The member states became responsible for supplying the market surveillance authorities with the resources necessary to enable them to achieve the provisions of the regulation. How market surveillance was to be organized, however, was still up to the respective member countries to decide.

In the Goods Package, the EU defined market surveillance as a control aimed at the economic operators (manufacturers, importers, distributors) and the CE mark was presented as a signal from the manufacturer to the authority in charge of market surveillance. Market surveillance authorities were now able to demand that economic operators provide documentation and information.

The extended requirements on 'independence' for the participating organizations in the Goods Package had now also reached to the principles of market surveillance. 'Market surveillance authorities shall carry out their duties independently, impartially and without bias' (765/2008/EC: 40).

In Sweden, the government chose to regulate market surveillance separately and not under the legislation from 2010 adapting Swedish law to the Goods Package with regard to accreditation and CE marking (SFS 2011:791). The 2010 government bill stated that: 'Through this system, the role of the authorities has become limited to encompass responsibility for the legislation and to ensure, by way of market surveillance, that the rules are followed in the market' (Prop. 2010/11:80: 38), but no proposals regarding how this market surveillance was to be organized were presented. In 2013, a ministry memorandum and government bill dealing specifically with market surveillance were issued. Market surveillance was now connected not only with controlling product safety, but also with promoting competition:

> Market surveillance is one component in a system aimed not only at keeping dangerous products off the market, but also at achieving a well-functioning internal market. In part serious actors are protected from unfair competition from actors whose products do not meet the applicable requirements, and in part effective market surveillance enables a system where products do not need to undergo costly *ex ante* controls conducted by public authorities. (Ds 2013:12: 29)

Since the legislative acts of the Goods Package related entirely to how market surveillance should be designed, the Swedish government took a decision to clarify which public authorities were responsible for market surveillance (Ds 2013:12). By creating a new piece of legislation on market surveillance, the government sought to create clarity and coherence in the regulation. The proposed bill led to a new statute on market surveillance and other related supervision (SFS 2014:1039). The new Swedish regulation also clarified that market surveillance was to be performed by state authorities, and the authorities commissioned to perform market surveillance were listed in an appendix. SFS 2014:1039 established that a market surveillance council (*Marknadskontrollrådet*) would be seated at Swedac, and that Swedac would serve as a national coordinating body.

EXTERNAL BORDER CONTROL

Market surveillance entails control of products already in the market, but the Goods Package also regulated control at the actual physical border of the market. The authorities given responsibility for monitoring the border to the internal market ('external border control') were also tasked with stopping products whose characteristics gave reason to believe that the product, when used or installed as intended, could pose a threat to health or safety. The same applied to products not accompanied by the documentation required by the legislation (such as technical documentation and declaration of conformity). The authorities responsible for the external border control – most often customs authorities – also gained the right to stop products with false or misleading CE marking (765/2008/EC). In Sweden, Swedish Customs was already one of the members of the Market Surveillance Council.

COOPERATION AT THE EUROPEAN LEVEL

By way of the Goods Package, the EU had constructed one accreditation organization in each member state. The idea was to keep them clearly distinguished from each other and they were not to compete, yet the EU needed a way to co-ordinate them. Therefore, the EU also sought to gather all of the accreditation organizations as members of a single organization (765/2008/EC). This organization would become the European cooperation for Accreditation (EA) in which membership became mandatory:

> The European cooperation for Accreditation (the EA), whose main mission is to promote a transparent and quality-led system for the evaluation of the competence of conformity assessment bodies throughout Europe, manages a peer evaluation system among national accreditation bodies from the Member States and other European countries. That system has proved to be efficient and to provide mutual confidence. The EA should, therefore, be the first body recognised under this Regulation and Member States should ensure that their national accreditation bodies seek and maintain membership of the EA for as long as it is so recognised. (765/2008/EC: 32, Recital 23)

The EA had existed since 1998 but through the Goods Package gained special and legal status, the same status as the standardization organizations (Interview 7). EA's presentation material depicts the quality 'infrastructure' in the form of a pyramid (see Figure 5.3).

At the top of the pyramid sits accreditation, with the levels connected by standards, shown as arrows pointing downward between the blocks. Standards form a bridge between accreditation and conformity assessment, and between conformity assessment and the components of the bottom block, such as

EA within the European Infrastructure

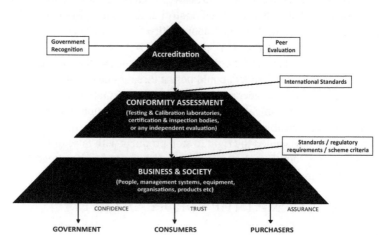

Source: Presentation material obtained during an interview at EA/UKAS.

Figure 5.3   The EA pyramid

management systems and products. The pyramid contains standards for both the forms of control and for the products. The result of the pyramid – or its basis – is written beneath the bottom layer: *Trust, Confidence* and *Assurance*; for *Government, Consumers* and *Purchasers*.

The idea of a pyramid (and with accreditation on top of it) was explained by one EA representative interviewed: '... in Europe we say from a philosophical point of view, you should only have one pinnacle to the structure. It is the ultimate level of control of the conformity assessment infrastructure' (Interview 13). This illustrates very clearly the idea of accreditation as top of the chain or the pyramid, above all other forms of control in the regime.

PEER ASSESSMENT AND MULTILATERAL AGREEMENTS

Because accreditation gained a more prominent role through the Goods Package, there was an expressed need for control also of the accreditation bodies. This was to be done through peer evaluation, giving the control regime yet another tool:

It is more important than ever that national accreditation bodies maintain the confidence of all stakeholders and regulators and are themselves regularly assessed by their peers in order to ensure their technical competency. This peer evaluation process must be transparent and accepted by all. (http://www.european-accreditation .org/role)

The main task of the EA was to evaluate the members and have peers evaluate them, that is, to evaluate the accreditation organizations' accreditation activities.

The guiding document, the Blue Guide, describes the peer evaluation system that EA was tasked with administrating as 'the cornerstone of the European accreditation system' (Blue Guide, Version 1.1: 92).

The peer evaluation was to be carried out on the basis of ISO standard 17011, and was intended as a way to ensure that the accreditation organizations were following the standard. In that membership in the EA built on ISO 17011, the status of the standard was even further strengthened. ISO 17011 and Regulation 765/2008 mutually presumed each other, and EA membership was based on the standard, a relationship described in one interview as 'circular':

So it's kind of a circular sort of thing. Because we accredited to 17011, because 17011 is considered a harmonized standard and has been published in the EU, then the presumption is that the bodies we say have successfully passed peer evaluation meet the evaluations of 765 .... You can go round and round. It's the way regulations are written.... (Interview 13)

I will return to this circularity later in the analysis, but already at this point it is worth adding that, within the EA, there was also a mutual recognition scheme for, in part, the accreditation organizations' accreditations (that had been approved by the EA through peer evaluation) and, in part, the accredited certification companies' certifications. This came to be called the multilateral agreement (MLA), and is described on the EA website as a *'passport to trade.'* The MLA constitutes yet another tool in the control regime. That is, under the agreement accreditation organizations would approve one another's accreditations and certifications carried out by certification companies that had been accredited by an EA member. The agreement built on five different levels, from accreditation to certification of management systems, that is, from the top to the bottom of the EA pyramid.[1]

The MLA knits the system together, and in one interview, the MLA was presented as very important for EA's activities: 'It's the end-product, everything is done so that the MLA will work' (Interview 7). The MLA gained legal status when the Goods Package was established.

COOPERATION AT THE INTERNATIONAL LEVEL

Through an agreement, EA was connected to its global equivalent: the International Accreditation Forum (IAF). The IAF became a coordinating organization for accreditation organizations, trade associations for certification companies, and other stakeholders in the field of accreditation and conformity assessment.[2] Regional accreditation body member organizations could also be given 'special recognition' by the IAF, which the EA had been granted. Besides the EA, there was also the IAAC (Inter-American Accreditation Cooperation), AFRAC (African Accreditation Cooperation), ARAC (Arab Accreditation Cooperation), PAC (Pacific Accreditation Cooperation) and SADCA (Southern Africa Development Community Cooperation in Accreditation) (www.european-accreditation.org/international-dimension).

One requirement for regional accreditation member organizations to receive special recognition by the IAF was that the regional organization have a program, like the EA's MLA, whereby the different members' accreditations were considered equivalent. The IAF would conduct an evaluation of its regional member organizations every four years.

Two important aims for IAF activities were to ensure that its members only accredited bodies that were authorized to perform the work they undertook and had no conflicts of interest, and to establish a program for mutual recognition. Once established, the mutual recognition program went by the name of the Multilateral Recognition Arrangement, MLA (http://www.iaf.nu//articles/ IAF_MLA/14), an important tool as it enabled the control regime to become global. To join the IAF, potential members were required to show that they intended to take part in the MLA. IAF's website also states that:

> IAF works to find the most effective way of achieving a single system that will allow companies with an accredited conformity assessment certificate in one part of the world, to have that certificate recognised elsewhere in the world. The objective of the MLA is that it will cover all accreditation bodies in all countries in the world …. (http://www.iaf.nu/articles/Role/7)

Thus, IAF's ambition was to create coherency among accreditation bodies and for all accreditations – and thereby all certifications – to maintain the same quality and therefore be accepted between countries, that is, a system that would cover the entire world.

When an accreditation organization joined the IAF and became a signatory to the MLA, this meant that the accreditation organization was required to accept certificates issued by certification companies accredited by other IAF members. The idea was that, with IAF promoting accreditation, the acceptance of certification would increase. The IAF slogan was 'certified once – accepted everywhere.' IAF's motivating arguments built on free trade and the elimination of technical trade barriers (www.iaf.nu). Such barriers could be the need to re-certify products or organizations in every new country where the certified entity was to operate or the certified product was to be sold.

Accreditation bodies that joined the IAF were given the right to use the IAF logo – a globe-like crest with surrounding text indicating MLA membership (www.iaf.nu/articles/The_MLA_Mark/45) (see Figure 5.4). Even certification companies that were accredited by an IAF member were entitled to use the logo, along with a logo from the accreditation body that had accredited them, for example, Swedac's logo with the three crowns.

Source: www.iaf.nu.

Figure 5.4   *The IAF logo*

The IAF's MLA should not be confused with the EA's MLA. The MLAs of the two organizations were similar, but not identical. However, the IAF agreement presupposed that an EA agreement had been drawn up. An accreditation body that was party to the EA's MLA was automatically recognized as party to the IAF's MLA (http://www.european-accreditation.org/iaf-and-ilac). A separate IAF MLA was drawn up with each specific accreditation body, but the actual controls that formed the basis for the agreements were handled by the respective regional accreditation organizations, for example, the EA.

World Accreditation Day

In addition to the MLA agreements, the IAF's work included selling the advantages of accreditation around the world. Every year in June accreditation organizations celebrate 'World Accreditation Day.' In Sweden, Swedac marks the occasion by inviting their customers (certification companies) and their customers' customers (certified companies) to celebrate the day with accreditation seminars and mingling. The themes change from year to year, for example, safe food and clean drinking water, or, as in 2011, international regulation (see Figure 5.5).

The idea behind World Accreditation Day has been to promote accreditation as it has come to be defined: a control of the competence of conformity assessment bodies. One aspect of the accreditation marketing work was to communicate that there was accreditation that can be trusted and accreditation that cannot be trusted. Accreditation was and is not a protected area: 'There is no law in this country that stops any other accreditation body from being set up. And indeed there are a number in this country that are set up' (Interview 13).

World Accreditation Day   9 June 2011

Supporting the work of regulators

Source: www.iaf.nu.

Figure 5.5   World Accreditation Day 2011

In the UK, an awareness campaign was initiated in an effort to raise awareness and explain the value of accreditation, in part for authorities purchasing accreditation, and in part for customers of certification companies (UKAS program proposal 2011–14, UKAS Awareness Campaign). One interviewee explained that accreditation companies that are not formally appointed nationally have lived off of accrediting without performing the control set out by the EU. Such accreditors were considered 'cowboys' (Interview 14) and, in the UK, the accreditation body wanted to create an awareness of the difference between proper accreditation versus improper accreditation:

> We would rather everything, all aspects of accreditation to come under the national accreditation body. ... Because that means it is properly .... when I say properly, it's been evaluated under the system that's open, that's transparent, that's covered under the legal aspects of Regulation 765. That's why we want it all to come under there. Not from a competition point of view, but to safeguard the end-user. (Interview 13)

Distinguishing 'proper' accreditation from 'other' accreditation and 'real' certification from 'other' certification appeared to be important: there is a difference between real certification and a certification company that 'certifies all of IKEA in a single afternoon' (Interview 3). The whole point of IAF, EA, accreditation and certification is, according to one interviewee, 'to ensure rigor in standards' (Interview 13) and to establish confidence in certification and accreditation. However, as put in another interview with a certification company, the recurring argument that confidence is essential to the system was made: 'there are laws and requirements left and right, everything all at once' and 'everything is connected' but, at the same time, 'if everyone had trusted each other, we wouldn't have been needed' (Interview 5).

This marks the end of my description of how the global system of accreditation, certification, market surveillance, self-conducted control and standards has come to be. In the next chapter, I explain how all this works as a global control regime.

NOTES

1. EA 2/02 2011 describes the five levels of the agreement:
    The first level is based on ISO 17011 and Regulation 765/2008/EC.
    The second level deals with the kind of conformity assessment the accreditation involved (e.g. inspection or certification).
    The third level is the standards that guide the conformity assessment (e.g. ISO 17020 or ISO 17021).
    The fourth level is the sector-specific standards that the bodies in level 2 (e.g. certification companies) are evaluated against.

The fifth level is the standards (e.g. ISO 9000 or ISO 14000 series) that the conformity assessment bodies use when assessing organizations (e.g. when certifying manufacturers).

2. In the field of laboratory accreditation, ILAC (International Laboratory Accreditation Cooperation) was formed.

6. Construction of a global control regime

In this chapter I analyse my field data in order to figure out how the national testing system in Sweden merged into the EU model that in turn was nestled in the global order of certification and accreditation, all were steps taken in the construction of the global control regime. The analysis is structured around the ideas and issues of organizations, organizing principles and control at a distance presented in Chapter 3. The first part of the analysis (this chapter) presents the components of the control regime and their juxtaposition. The second part of the analysis relates the findings to ideas about control from a distance and about the organizing of and among organizations.

I begin the chapter with a thematic summary of the control regime's development from 1972 to 2014.

SUMMARY OF THE CONTROL REGIME'S DEVELOPMENT 1972–2014

In its design, the Swedish national system for testing and inspection (the National Testing System) founded in 1972 was a wholly public-law system. All of the rules (authority-issued regulations supported in legislation) were created by the state, and all of the controls (at national testing sites) were carried out by the state.

During the 1980s, the Swedish government opened the field to other types of rules as well. Official investigations and government bills dealt more and more with international standards. Standards were presented as voluntary rules, the purpose of which was to create consistent dimensions and definitions, mainly of products and organizational processes. When the discussion of standards began, other forms of control also began to appear on the agenda. In the case of the Swedish government, discussions centered mainly around certification, accreditation and 'self-conducted monitoring'.

These discussions had two main points of departure. One was that views on the public sector and of the role the state should play changed in the 1980s. In conjunction with this, the National Testing System was criticized for being rigid and creating bureaucracy. The second was that a Europeanization of the public sector was occurring alongside preparations for joining the EEA in 1991, at the same time as international trade increasingly became a part of the discussion. These tendencies promoted the argument for introducing and increasing the use of standards. *Flexibility, rationality, competitiveness* and *internationalization* are recurring concepts in the field data.

When Sweden became a member of the EEA, the National Testing System was decommissioned and replaced by the then-existing EC model for control: the New Approach and the Global Approach. The components of these approaches included standards, certification and accreditation, self-conducted monitoring, and market surveillance. In the field data, standards were described as the bones or foundation of the system, and the main purpose of the system as a whole was to ensure compliance with those standards. Standards became the actual control instrument of the system, controlling products, manufacturers through internal control, the certification companies, and the accreditation organizations. With the introduction of the standards, quality assurance was revamped as the form of control, thereby moving the focus of control from the *physical product* to the manufacturing *process*. Quality assurance became a tool that had to do with manufacturers' internal control, the certification companies (when they were accredited) and the accreditation organizations. In the context of standards and quality assurance, the same control instrument (standards) began to be used by both the controllers and the controlled.

The objects of control were organizational processes: management systems and documented procedures. Over time, accreditation begins to be defined as a control aimed only at organizations.

In the control regime it was a specific type of standards that came to constitute control instruments, namely, the standards that were and are created by the standardization organizations ISO and CEN. It was the EU Commission that approved the standards for publishing and the standardization organizations were thereby not responsible for the control instruments they created.

In the early days of the control regime, the dividing lines between certification and accreditation, and between public and commercial control were not distinct. The Goods Package served to clarify the boundaries between the tools of the control regime. Certification and accreditation were controlled by different standards (ISO 17011 and ISO 17021, respectively) and were to be kept separate, on different 'levels'. The EU expended great effort to create a specific role for accreditation, deciding that public authorities would not engage in commercial control activities such as certification.

A new tool was also added: through the European cooperation for Accreditation (EA), accreditation organizations would evaluate each other using standards as the control instrument. The controllers hereby began to control each other. By way of the International Accreditation Forum (IAF) and agreements that built on the controls of the accreditation organizations and the EA, accreditation and certification, as tools, were able to gain a global reach.

THE COMPONENTS OF THE CONTROL REGIME

In Chapter 3 I presented an analytical model based on the idea that a control regime is made up of a number of components that together enable control at a distance. The components of the analytical model are: (1) an organization that creates control instruments, (2) control instruments and manuals for the control instruments, (3) tools used to control, and (4) objects that are controlled.

The control regime is constructed using standards as the control instrument. To interpret the standards, there are guiding documents, laws, regulations and directives – which serve as manuals for the standards. To ensure compliance with standards, there are a number of tools in the form of different forms of control and organizations that verify that the standards are followed. The controls are aimed at organizations and organizational processes. Because the objects of control in the control regime are organizations, organizations are both the tools for control and the objects controlled, a discussion I will return to in the next chapters.

As presented in Chapter 3, I build my analysis on how the control regime is constructed, based on four components:

The organizations that create the control instruments. Those who create the control instruments in the control regime are the standards organizations ISO and CEN. These organizations create standards that control the objects of control. The EU and the Swedish government create manuals explaining how the instruments are to be used.

Control instruments in the form of a specific type of standard and manuals. In the control regime, different standards are used. The most fundamental for the sake of the control regime is the ISO 9001, which is a generically designed standard to apply to quality assurance in various organizations. ISO 9001 is used as an instrument to control the internal control carried out by manufacturers, but certification companies and accreditation organizations also use ISO 9001 for their own activities. The ISO 17021 standard is an instrument used to control certification organizations. ISO 17011 is an instrument to control accreditation organizations. Various product standards regulate products and their production. The manuals take the form of written directives, regulations, guiding documents for manufacturers, importers and distributors, and laws and other legal statutes. These manuals describe how the control regime's instruments (standards) are to be used and how the control regime's activities are to be performed: for example, EU directives describe how accreditation is to be carried out with respect to certification, and the market surveillance legislation describes how market surveillance is to be carried out. Manuals help the objects controlled to interpret their tasks, but the tasks themselves are given in standards.

Tools used to control. The toolbox of the control regime contains a set of controls such as accreditation, certification, self-conducted monitoring, market surveillance, and membership. There are, in addition, a number of organizations that serve as tools, such as membership organizations, accreditation organizations, certification organizations and market surveillance organizations, to control other organizations. The tools are used to ensure compliance with the standards.

Objects of control. In the control regime, it is formal organizations that are controlled. The organizations controlled are member organizations, accreditation organizations, certification organizations, market surveillance organizations, manufacturers, importers and distributors.

To summarize, the control regime is made up of four components: creators of control instruments; control instruments and manuals for control instruments; tools used to control; and objects of control. How the components relate to one another is decisive for the ability of the regime to obtain global control. This juxtaposing is addressed in the following.

JUXTAPOSITION OF THE COMPONENTS

In Chapter 3 I wrote that, in order to understand how the control regime has been constructed, I need a way to study organizing without pre-conditions, a way that does not 'lock' organizing into the formal organization as an entity. By employing the concept of action nets, organizing becomes a process of connecting actions and events, rather than viewing organizing as a product of organizations. I also worked on the assumption that the organizing principles analytically assigned to the formal organization as an institutionalized entity can serve equally well as principles for understanding organizing of and among organizations, as organizing within them.

In Chapter 3, I also wrote that control becomes possible when the components are positioned in relation to one another in a certain way. Based on Law (1986) and Law and Singleton (2005), I called this the 'juxtaposition' of the components. How the components are juxtaposed determines how the control regime functions – it is through this juxtaposing that control is made possible, otherwise the components would merely be a set of components. The juxtaposition of the components is an empirical question for every control regime. In the control regime I studied, standards need accreditation and certification in order to work, and accreditation becomes accreditation in relation to certification – without certification, accreditation loses the specific meaning it has been given in the control regime. The organizing principles have guided the analysis of how the components of the control regime are juxtaposed. For example, I have interpreted the distinction between accreditation and certification as

Table 6.1   *Four principles behind the juxtaposition of the components*

A. Division of labor	B. Chain-like linkage	C. A hub	D. A unity
A1. Open systems	B1. Principle of presumption	C1. Accreditation principles	D1. Words: package, approach, system, coherence, clarity, transparency
A2. Specialization	B2. Controlling others, not oneself (except manufacturers)	C2. Confidence argument	D2. Boundaries to the environment
A3. Independent organizations	B3. Membership builds on more organizations	C3. Both controlled by and control others using standards	D3. Agreements that tie accreditation, certification and standards together
A4. Hierarchy		C4. Coordination	D4. Common terminology
		C5. Coordination of coordination	D5. Own logo

a form of division of labor, and the 'levels' between certification and accreditation as a hierarchy of sorts.

Table 6.1 consists of four columns, each representing one of the juxtaposed principles that determine the control regime's control: the principle of division of labor, the principle of a chain-like linkage, the principle of a hub, and the principle of a unity. The principles are presented in more detail in Table 6.1 and the text that follows.

A. DIVISION OF LABOR

The global control regime juxtaposes the components in relation to one another such that it creates 'open systems' (A1), such that it creates specialization (A2), through the idea of autonomous and independent organizations (A3), and in that there must be different levels in a hierarchy of sorts (A4). Together, open systems, specialization, the independent organizations and the hierarchy constitute a division of labor in the global control regime.

A1. Open Systems

In the Global Approach notified bodies would compete with each other in what was called an 'open system for conformity assessment'. Everyone can take part if they are able to show that they comply with the relevant standard (control instrument). In Sweden, the Global Approach was called 'the open system for testing and inspection,' where 'open' means that the system is open to many providers, who compete with each other. The open system was explicitly motivated by the fact that there were to be many controlling organizations to choose from.

The modular system also opened the system for more controlling organizations to participate: the modules allow notified bodies to do the same thing, that is, to work in a coherent manner when applying the modules, so that a manufacturer would be subject to the same assessment regardless of which notified body it went to. The system would thereby provide more notified bodies for the manufacturer to choose from.

Having an open system with several participant organizations was a deliberate strategy. The idea of creating a central organization under which control activities in the control regime could be gathered was rejected on three occasions: once at the Global Approach's inception in 1989, when the EU discussed the option of handling conformity assessment centrally at the European Community level, and a second and third time, in 1994 and then again in 2004, when the Swedish government considered gathering all market surveillance under one central market surveillance authority. Neither the European central control organization nor the Swedish central market surveillance authority came to be. In the EU, this was because a central organization for conformity assessment was seen as creating another layer of bureaucracy for the internal market.

Overall, the open system, including the modular system and the decision to not introduce a central EU organization for conformity assessment or a Swedish central market surveillance authority, makes it possible for more controlling organizations to participate in the control regime, which is in turn a precondition for the control regime being able to divide the labor between them.

A2. Specialization

The motivation for the National Testing System was a desire to divide testing and inspection between seven national testing facilities, where each was to specialize in their particular area.

When the Global Approach and the principle of open systems was introduced in 1989 (1991 in Sweden), it created a space for more controlling organizations (see A1), and each organization specialized in a single task. This was a gradual development: when the new control forms of self-conducted monitoring, certification and accreditation were introduced in Sweden in the 1980s, no major distinction was made between certification, accreditation and control by an authority. With the introduction of the Global Approach, however, it became important to distinguish between the different organizations: market surveillance authorities, notified bodies (certification organizations), accreditation organizations, standards organizations and manufacturers were to engage in only one thing each. This was reflected in the certification organizations being given a specially scripted role in the Global Approach, in that they came to be called 'notified bodies' and based their control on New Approach directives. The Global Approach separated certification from control by an authority by specifying that authorities were not to engage in certification activities. It was made clear that authorities should not engage in commercial control. The role of the authorities was to be refined and they were not to impede on the commercial control market.

With the Goods Package (2008), the definition of the tools became even more explicit: the activities of accreditation organizations were to be separate from the activities of certification organizations, with the distinction being that accreditation was not to be a commercial activity, whereas certification was. Accreditation was also distinguished from other forms of conformity assessment in that accreditation could only be performed on (other) organizations. Notified bodies and notifying bodies became regulated in relation to each other; manufacturers, importers and distributors were assigned different tasks in the supply chain. The activities of market surveillance authorities were distinguished from other control by stressing that market surveillance was to be carried out *after* market entry of a product and be conducted by a public authority, a kind of specialization of control.

In the market surveillance regulation (SFS 2014:1039) (i.e. a 'manual'), the government sought to clarify the boundaries between different authorities' areas of responsibility, that is, clear boundaries regarding which authority would do what were seen as necessary so that each authority could specialize in control of its particular area.

The concept of *grey zones* was used to describe cases where the lines were blurred and needed clarification, both between manufacturers, importers and distributors (and their obligations to one another) and between the areas of responsibility of different market surveillance authorities. Clearer boundaries would lead to specialization.

Directive 98/34 clarified that standardization was to be handled by specifically designated standardization organizations and not by the EU or member states' national authorities. In this way the standardization organizations became specialized in creating standards.

As a whole, specialization was created in the control regime by the control tools and objects of control each specializing in a single task: market surveillance, certification or accreditation. Manufacturers, importers and distributors became clearly defined and specialized to their role in the supply chain. Only the standardization organizations can create the control instrument – the standards, which is itself also a kind of specializing.

A3. Independent Organizations

The division of labor in the control regime also occurs by the requirement that the controlling organizations and the organizations controlled must remain 'independent' from each other – maintaining a separation between them helps to clarify their tasks in relation to each other. Earlier, even the national testing sites were required to perform independent controls, which was the motivation for the state handling the control, since state authorities and state-owned companies were assumed to be independent of commercial interests. This requirement changed with the Global Approach and the Goods Package. The requirement for independence remained, but it no longer motivated state control.

When the Global Approach was evaluated in 2006, the open system was described as a model in which 'independent' and 'autonomous' organizations compete with one another to perform conformity assessments.

When the Goods Package was introduced, the independence requirement applied to even more of the tools: notified bodies, notifying bodies and market surveillance authorities were to be independent from those they controlled. They were to be impartial and objective, they were not permitted to have close relations with the bodies they controlled, and they were not permitted to provide consulting services that could affect the independent relationship with the controlled party. Authorities could not engage in commercial control as it was thought that confidence in their activities would suffer if a conflict of interest existed between them and the objects they controlled.

The Goods Package established that accreditation was not a commercial activity and could not be operated on a for-profit basis. Accreditation was to be performed by authorities or by organizations with authority status. This would guarantee the independence of accreditation.

A4. Hierarchy

The concept of *level* appears in the field data when referring to the accreditation organizations' relation to the certification organizations. In one interview, accreditation is described as 'one level above certification,' or that accreditation is a control that is further away from society than certification. Emphasis was placed on this notion, it was the levels that were important. When the accreditation organizations began to be controlled by the EU, the motivation cited was that, in order for the control systems to become international, a level of control above the member countries was needed – accreditation was seen as being one level above national controls.

The relation of accreditation organizations and certification organizations on different levels was created when the Global Approach was introduced and the tasks of certification and the tasks of accreditation were clearly distinguished from each other. The levels were further clarified with the Goods Package in 2008.

The illustration of the control regime as a pyramid in Chapter 5 (Figure 5.4) is perhaps the clearest depiction of the control regime as a hierarchical construction – with accreditation organizations on the top, and certification companies and other forms of conformity assessment below.

B. CHAIN-LIKE LINKAGE

The components of the control regime are linked to each other like a chain. The connections occur in three ways: by the principle of presumption (B1), by the controlling organizations controlling others, not themselves (except manufacturers who control themselves) (B2), and by membership in the EA and IAF (B3).

B1. The Principle of Presumption

Mandatory EU directives are linked to standards written by the standardization organizations using the principle of presumption. When the standards are published in EU's official journal, they become harmonized and are given a legal basis. The standardization organizations write standards on the mandate provided in Directive 98/34. The principle of presumption, established by the Global Approach, applies to both product standards and standards for forms of control. If a manufacturer is in compliance with a product manufacturing standard, it is presumed also to be in compliance with the specific New Approach product directive. If an accreditation organization complies with ISO 17011 (which controls the work of accreditation organizations), that accreditation organization is also considered to meet the EU requirements laid out for accreditation organizations in the legal instruments of the Goods Package (in particular 765/2008/EC). These linkages provide standards as a control instrument legal basis and applies to several tools in the control regime giving the standards a rather profound impact.

The links lead further to the coordinating European organization, the EA, because the principle of presumption forms the basis of EA membership. If the EA accepts, based on peer evaluation, that an accreditation organization meets the requirements of ISO 17011, the accreditation organization is thereby regarded as being in compliance with the requirements of Regulation 765/2008/EC (and vice versa) and can become a member of the EA, a relationship referred to as 'circular' in one of the interviews.

Together, the standards and the directives are written in such a way that they build on, presume and link to each other. Every control instrument (standard) requires a manual (directive). Through these linkages, the control instrument of standards can be used across the entire control regime.

B2. Controlling Others, Not Oneself (Except Manufacturers)

The control performed by the different tools is the control of other organizations, with the one exception of the self-conducted monitoring of manufacturers.

That control activities apply to organizations other than the controller is a consistent feature throughout the entire control regime: the IAF's agreement applies to the EA or national accreditation organizations, the EA's assignment and work applies to accreditation organizations through the peer evaluations the EA is tasked with performing, accreditation organizations accredit certification organizations (i.e. an organization cannot accredit itself), certification organizations certify the manufacturer's self-monitoring (i.e. an organization cannot certify itself), the market surveillance authorities control the manufacturer and the manufacturer's products (the manufacturer can not perform market surveillance of its own products), and the notified bodies are given the task of controlling others, not themselves. Manufacturers, importers and distributors are tasked with being able to account for others in the supply chain that they buy from or sell to, and controlling that the organization ahead of them in the chain has fulfilled its tasks.

B3. Membership Builds on Other Organizations

The linking of tools, objects of control and control instruments is seen also in how membership in the EA and the IAF is designed. Membership in these organizations builds on five levels, where each level involves control of an organization: for an accreditation organization to become an approved member of the EA, it must be able to demonstrate that it follows ISO 17011 for accreditation, that it only accredits certification organizations in compliance with ISO 17021 for certification companies, and that the certification organization in turn performs certification in a proper manner according to the relevant standards such as ISO 9001. Membership in the IAF, further, builds on approved membership in the EA. The IAF slogan is therefore 'certified once – accepted everywhere' and not 'accredited once – accepted everywhere,' because accreditation is relevant only when certification is taken into account.

C. A HUB

A hub is a central point where things come together or changeovers occur. In the global control regime the accreditation organizations are made into hubs. This is done in five ways: with the Goods Package principles for accreditation

(C1), with the confidence argument (C2), by the accreditation organizations both being controlled by and controlling others based on standards (C3), through coordination (C4), and through coordination of coordination (C5).

C1. Principles for Accreditation Organizations

The Goods Package and Directive 765/2008/EC presented four principles for accreditation organizations:

- accreditation is not to be operated on a commercial basis,
- accreditation is to be performed by an organization with public authority status (either by a public authority or by a company with an agreement with the member state granting the accreditation organization authority status),
- there is to be only one accreditation organization per country, and
- the accreditation organization is to be formally appointed by the government of that member country.

These principles clarify the accreditation organization's special role and function in the control regime and establish that accreditation is different from other tools like certification. In the interviews in my study, in EA's presentation material, and in the legislative acts of the Goods Package, accreditation is described as the top of a pyramid with other forms of control underneath. Accreditation is the last level and is emphasized as possessing a special value, a special status, 'the last pinnacle to the structure'. Accreditation is not included the concept of *conformity assessment*, but is regarded as something separate.

C2. Confidence

In the National Testing System the concept of *confidence* was used as an argument for having the state operate testing and control.

Toward the end of the 1980s, confidence began to be considered in connection with accreditation – confidence in foreign testing and control would be created through accreditation. The emphasis on the value of confidence for testing and control grew when Sweden was to adapt to international systems, and at the end of the 1980s the purpose of accreditation was said to be just that – to create confidence.

In the Global Approach, the EU also used confidence as an argument for the importance of a common organization to ensure compliance with the standards – it was important for the Global Approach to generate confidence and confidence is a core and key concept in the Commission's communication on the Global Approach.

The concept of confidence was also used with the Goods Package, though now explicitly with the accreditation organizations specifically in mind. It was the activities of the accreditation organizations that were to create confidence – in part for those accreditation activities, and in part for what was being accredited, for example, certification organizations, which in turn were to create confidence for the internal market. In the figure that depicts the regime as a pyramid (Figure 5.4) the word 'trust' appears under the pyramid's base. Thus, depending on how you look at it, trust is either what is holding the whole pyramid up or what the work described in the pyramid should lead to. The confidence argument has thereby been shifted from having to do with test results (in the National Testing System) to having to do with accreditation (of certification activities), and accreditation is thus made into a hub for trust within the control regime.

C3. Both Controlled by and Controlling Others Based on Standards

The accreditation organizations are controlled by the control instrument for accreditation organizations, ISO standard 17011. The task of an accreditation organization is to accredit other organizations based on standards. The accreditation organization is thus controlled by a standard (ISO 17011) in order to control other organizations based on standards (e.g. certification companies based on ISO 17021), which in turn control yet others based on standards (e.g. ISO 9001). Swedac illustrated this with a diagram (Figure 5.2) in which Swedac appears alongside ISO 17011, below which other standards are shown. The diagram illustrates how that in Swedac – as in all of the other accreditation bodies in the EU – all of the standards of the control regime are nestled together at a central point, a hub.

C4. Coordination

During the development of the control regime, more and more tasks were assigned to the accreditation organizations, in Sweden to the authority that is now called Swedac. Swedac is responsible for accrediting, serves as a notifying authority for the notified bodies, and chairs and serves as coordinator for the Market Surveillance Council, which in turn coordinates the market surveillance. Swedac became the national accreditation body through Regulation 765/2008/EC and thereby also Sweden's representative to the EA and the IAF. With the introduction of the Goods Package, Swedac was given the sole right to accredit in the country. In Sweden, Swedac is the coordinating hub for the European and global control systems. There are 'Swedacs' in every EU country and in countries around the world, such as UKAS in the UK and Danak in Denmark.

C5. Coordination of Coordination

The Goods Package made the EA a coordinating organization for accreditation organizations in the EU, where the coordination occurs by way of membership. All nationally appointed accreditation organizations in the EU must belong to the EA. EA membership builds on the MLA agreements whereby members evaluate each other through several steps. Regional equivalents to the EA with various acronyms can be found around the world (e.g. IAAC, AFRAC, ARAC, PAC, SADCA). Coordination of the EA and these regional organizations occurs through the IAF and its global MLA. As the accreditation organizations coordinate certification in the control regime, this makes the EA coordination of coordination and, in turn, the IAF coordination of coordination (via the EA) of coordination (the accreditation organizations).

As the control regime developed, from the National Testing Sites to World Accreditation Day and the UK awareness campaign, stress was placed on the need for a single system for certification and accreditation, and for the parties involved to avoid creating parallel systems for control. The IAF and the EA thus also coordinate accreditation by promoting accreditation through various PR campaigns, like World Accreditation Day, that explain there is only one true system for accreditation.

D. UNITY

Attempts to depict and portray the control regime as a unified global system is a recurring feature in the field data. The control regime is described by: words that imply a single whole – package, method, global and system – and with arguments like coherence, clarity and transparency (D1); the idea that the control regime should have boundaries to its environment (D2); agreements that link standards, certification and accreditation (D3); the use of a common terminology in the control regime (D4); and the control regime having its own logo (D5).

D1. Package, Method, Global and System

Concepts such as *coherence* and *clarity* have been used to describe, or to advocate change in all of the three models: the National Testing System, the Global Approach, and the Goods Package.

In the first bills from 1972 and 1974, the Swedish government argued there was a need for a coherent approach to deal with testing and control. The National Testing System was to rectify a fragmented organization of the field. During the 1980s, descriptions of non-official testing and control operations (i.e. control performed by bodies other than a public authority or national testing site) used terms like 'complicated' and 'incomplete.'

When the Global Approach was launched in 1989, the intention was to create a transparent and complete structure for control, with clear and coherent rules, with insight into the regulatory work of the different countries (by means of Directive 98/34/EC, among others). The Global Approach was to be 'coherent' and 'transparent,' terms that appear repeatedly in the Commission's communication (89/C 267/03).

Presented in the early 1990s, the modular system was a way of creating coherence in the activities that made up different forms of conformity assessment.

The purpose of the Goods Package was to create more coherence in the Global Approach. These coherent rules would be raised to a level above the member countries. When market surveillance was reformed to adapt to the Goods Package, greater coherence in the market surveillance activities was sought.

The names *Global Approach, New Approach, Open System* and *Goods Package* indicate that the control regime is made up of components, capable of forming a whole or being a system, capable of having its own approach and being seen as a package. In following with this the legal framework of Decision 768/2008/EC was created in the Goods Package as a rule for how other rules should be written, the ambition being that all New Approach directives would be the same: coherent and explicit.

The control instrument of standards was used to create coherence in several ways. The Global Approach introduced standards with the aim of simplifying a common terminology, coordinated measurements, definitions, and specifications of functions and characteristics. The purpose of the New Approach was to harmonize these standards in the EU.

The Global Approach and the Goods Package required clear and unequivocal documentation. All of these activities were to be based on standards. When Sweden's Open System for testing and control was evaluated in 2006, the conclusion was that the only thing needed in order to apply the Open System was a clearly formulated requirements document against which independent organizations could conduct their assessments and arrive at the same results. This requirements document was a standard.

When the EA depicted the regime as a pyramid or triangle composed of different parts, the parts are linked together with standards (Figure 5.4). The diagram illustrates the control regime as a coherent entity, held together by standards, a kind of organizational chart of the control regime.

D2. Boundaries to the Environment

The National Testing System, the Global Approach and the Goods Package have in common that they created a framework for control but not the actual requirements for the products on EU's internal market. The Goods Package and Regulation 764/2008/EC created the legal basis for products that do not fall within the framework of the New Approach directives. This means that the member countries are not permitted to write rules for products that can constitute a barrier to the free movement of goods. Regulation 764/2008/EC gave the EU the ability to control products that fell outside the New Approach as well, thereby clarifying that there was an 'inside,' the internal market where products could circulate freely, and an 'outside,' controlled by a special directive. It is also easy to determine which products are included in the control regime by observing whether or not they carry the CE mark.

When the EU, by means of the Goods Package, began to control importers, the importers became the border guards: importers were defined as the organization that brings products from the outside market across the border into EU's internal market.

With the Goods Package came also discussion of 'enforcement at external borders' and, in following, when market surveillance was reformed in Sweden, Swedish Customs Authority was elected into the Market Surveillance Council. Swedish Customs Authority has the necessary competence for border enforcement and control of the import of products from countries outside the EU. Together with the importers, Swedish Customs Authority creates a border control to markets and countries outside the internal market.

D3. Agreements that Tie the System Together

According to Decision 764/2008/EC, the principle of mutual recognition applies to both products and forms of control. The principle of mutual recognition constitutes a kind of agreement whereby the organizations that fall under the Goods Package undertake to accept all other controls performed by accredited certification organizations. All of the activities conducted under this agreement – regardless of where they are carried out – must be interchangeable with each other.

However, that which is called the Global Approach or Goods Package within the EU does not reach beyond the EU. Therefore, for the control regime to be able to become global required the IAF organization. Through MLA agreements between the EA and the accreditation organizations as well as between the EA and the IAF, the regime is able to attain a global reach since the organizations that belong to the EA or IAF accept one another's accreditations. The agreements interlink the control instruments, the control tools and the objects of control, all around the globe.

The ambition to tie all accreditation around the world together into one whole, with a symbol that resembles the globe wrapped in standards and images of things that work because of standards, was illustrated when the IAF launched World Accreditation Day. The 2011 World Accreditation Day slogan was 'Supporting the work of regulators,' which is precisely what accreditation under the agreements does (Figure 5.6). IAF's slogan is 'Certified once – accepted everywhere,' and the organization's objective is to create, by way of agreements, an infrastructure for accreditation organizations and certification organizations that spans the globe. To aid in this ambition, the IAF has its logo – which also resembles a globe (Figure 5.5). The logo enables member organizations to show that they have entered an agreement with the IAF and thereby belong to the global control regime.

D4. Common Terminology

The legislative acts of the Goods Packages provide a list of the terminology used, defining the activities initiated by the Global Approach and the New Approach. That the same terms were assigned different meanings in different members states was seen as problematic; this made it more difficult for a control regime where the objects and tools of control were to be coherent and easily comparable. The decision-makers in the EU sought a higher level of coherence in the meaning of the terms used. The listed terms became a kind of glossary, a check list, for the control regime's internal communication – the concepts were to have the same meaning throughout the global control regime.

D5. Its Own Logo

When the National Testing System was abandoned and the Global Approach came into practice, Sweden also introduced the control regime's logo, the CE mark. In the Goods Package the CE mark was presented as the end result of many activities. The CE mark thus materializes and symbolizes the control regime as a coherent whole. The legislated regulations stipulated that only one mark was to be used as the control regime mark. The CE mark was not to be confused with others. The CE mark was to be visible, durable, and clearly legible.

It was also stressed that the CE mark was not a consumer mark but a signal from the manufacturer to market surveillance authorities that the product marked complied with the set requirements. This tied the control regime together. The CE mark constitutes a means of communication between the organizations in the control regime, carrying a meaning that they have agreed on.

The CE mark is the control regime's logo within the EU. The IAF logo makes it possible for the control regime to communicate globally.

To sum up, control in the control regime is constructed according to four juxtaposed principles: (1) the principle of the division of labor, (2) the principle of a chain-like linkage, (3) the principle of a hub, and (4) the principle of a unity.

In the next chapter I analyse the organizing of the control regime based on a discussion of control at a distance and a discussion of the organizing of and among organizations.

7.   Control and distance

In this chapter I continue my analysis of the construction of the global control regime. The control regime's construction is discussed in relation to the concepts of *control at a distance* and the *organizing of* and *organizing among* organizations presented in Chapter 3.

THE CONTROL REGIME AND CONTROL AT A DISTANCE

In Chapter 3 I wrote that the concept of organizations' surrounding *environment* – that which is assumed to exist outside organizations – can be linked to the concept of *distance*. The advantage of making this connection is that distance lends itself to being problematized in more ways than the concept of environment. Distance can be cognitive, geometric, temporal, spatial and/or relational. The concept of distance can above all also lead to ideas of how control at a distance occurs, which is relevant for analysing the control regime.

The analytical model presented in Chapter 3 stems in large part from Law's (1986) model for how control at a distance is made possible. Law's thinking was that people, objects and inscriptions (texts) together create control. People, objects and inscriptions are components of control at a distance, but their various combinations also create the distance that is to be controlled. Distance is, as also noted in Chapter 3, an effect rather than an absolute state (Law and Mol 2008).

In Chapter 6 I stated that standards are the control regime's control instruments, and that organizations are both the regime's tools and objects of control. I also discussed the juxtaposition (Law 1986; Law and Singleton 2005) of the components in the control regime. I present the table from that chapter (Table 6.1) again here as Table 7.1, to interpret the principles behind the juxtapositions of the components. In this chapter I interpret the table based on Law's notion that, to make control at a distance possible, the center and the periphery must be in contact so that the communication between them remains unbroken. The global control regime is also interpreted based on Law's idea of the ability of functioning control at a distance to incorporate the environment so that the control can be enduring and strong (Law 1986). The division of labor, the linking of organizations, a coordinating hub and description of the control regime as a coherent unity are the ways in which the control regime

Table 7.1   Four principles behind the juxtaposition of the components

A. Division of labor	B. Chain-like linkage	C. A hub	D. A unity
A1. Open systems	B1. Principle of presumption	C1. Accreditation principles	D1. Words: package, approach, global, system, coherence, clarity, transparency
A2. Specialization	B2. Controlling others, not oneself (except manufacturers)	C2. Confidence argument	D2. Boundaries to the environment
A3. Independent organizations	B3. Membership builds on more organizations	C3. Both controlled by and control others using standards	D3. Agreements that tie accreditation, certification and standards together
A4. Hierarchy		C4. Coordination	D4. Common terminology
		C5. Coordination of coordination	D5. Own logo

creates this unbroken communication and incorporates the environment. I show how in the following.

UNBROKEN COMMUNICATION

In the control regime the components are juxtaposed so that the communication between them remains unbroken. This is achieved above all by means of standards. All of the organizations in the control regime are controlled by standards. The organizations (except the manufacturer) then have the task of controlling some other organization by means of standards so that contact is created locally to globally – the work of the global IAF builds on EA agreements with the accreditation organizations that control the certification companies that control the manufacturers that control their own production, a control that is required in order for the products to be sold around the global. Standards create 'glocal' control and 'glocal' communication (Robertson 1992). And because standards are used both locally and globally, unbroken communication throughout the control regime is made possible – the same control instrument can be used no matter *where* it is used.

Unbroken communication is also made possible by how the organizations in the control regime are linked together (Juxtaposition B). Every object that is controlled – every organization – has the task of controlling the next object (except the manufacturer). A chain of organizations is thus formed, where the organizations link to each other, creating contact between the organizations of the control regime, so that the components are in constant contact with each other. Which organization links to which in the chain is controlled through a division of labor (Juxtaposition A).

Also the hubs of the control regime (Juxtaposition C) help to promote unbroken communication. A hub is where the communication comes together and interconnects – it is through the accreditation organizations that the IAF, EA and certification organizations are in contact with each other. The accreditation organizations provide, in addition, coordination for market surveillance and registering notified bodies. The accreditation organizations thereby become communication hubs of sorts.

The articulated idea of a coherent whole – the principle of a unity (Juxtaposition D) – creates a common language shared by the organizations of the global control regime. Having a common terminology means that words and concepts don't need to be translated between the different organizations of the global control regime, meaning the communication need not be interrupted or distorted. The principle of unity also promotes unbroken communication in that the parties involved have an idea of what is internal and what is external – that is, what can be communicated with and what can't. For example, products from outside the internal market are easily identified in that they lack the CE mark.

Together, the division of labor, the linking of control objects, the coordinating hubs and the creation of a coherent unity create the unbroken communication in the control regime.

INCORPORATING THE ENVIRONMENT

For a control regime to be able to control at a distance and cover large areas requires methods to incorporate the environment. In the global control regime, this is manifested in the work to describe and shape the control regime as a unity (Juxtaposition D). The principle of mutual recognition enables the regime to incorporate also things that previously lay outside the regime, that is, products not covered by the New Approach's directives, or accreditations and certifications carried out by organizations outside the Goods Package. With the IAF and EA's work with MLA agreements the environment is incorporated to an extent that makes the control regime global and the tools and objects of control 'accepted everywhere' (the IAF slogan). Linking components together like a chain (Juxtaposition B) is also a way of incorporating the environment – by being in contact with one another, the organizations are able to cover greater distances without losing contact with the control regime or each other. They do not become isolated satellites or ships lost in unknown waters, but parts of a chain.

This was also the reason why the National Testing System was unable to become 'accepted everywhere' – the National Testing System was not built on standards but on national and state-conducted *ex ante* controls. The system was therefore unable to reach beyond Sweden's borders and thus unable to incorporate a larger environment.

The division of labor (Juxtaposition A) allows the control regime to create functions that make it possible to control areas outside the EU as well: self-conducted monitoring enables control of the manufacturer even when the manufacturer is outside the EU's boundaries. The importer and the distributor, which are as per the control regime's definition within the borders of the EU, are given the task of ensuring that the manufacturer carries out its internal control; self-conducted control is not bound by place. By dividing the work between the manufacturer, the importer and the distributor along a supply chain, larger areas than just the internal market are incorporated.

To sum up, the juxtaposition of the components (division of labor, a hub, chain-like linkage, and description of a coherent unity) enables the control regime to become global. The components' juxtapositions make it possible for communication in the regime to remain unbroken and for the environment to be incorporated so that the regime can cover larger areas. The importance of these aspects for functioning control at a distance was noted by Law in his work from 1986. But the construction of the global control regime is also characterized by aspects that Law (1986) did not discuss but that I have found in the field data. These aspects are elaborated on below.

DISTANCE AND THE ORGANIZING OF ORGANIZATIONS

In terms of organizing, four aspects of the control regime's construction have bearing on the ideas of control at a distance presented in Chapter 3. The first is that control at a distance is created in the global control regime through *bureaucratic organizing principles*. The bureaucratic organizing principles create control *among* the organizations of the control regime and not just *inside* them. The second aspect is that the formal organizations (in the sense of legal persons) in the global control regime cannot merely be interpreted as objects, but also as *standardized* and *interchangeable*. The third aspect is that the control regime creates control that *absorbs distance*. And the fourth aspect is that, unlike Law's case, the control regime is characterized by there being *no one* with a clear mandate *to control* the regime as a whole.

CONTROL AT A DISTANCE BY WAY OF ORGANIZING PRINCIPLES

In my model I made the assumption that the organizing principles, referred to in previous literature as *bureaucratic* or *administrative* principles, should also be found *outside* and *among* organizations and not just *inside* them. Hall (1963) argued that bureaucracy was not an absolute state that either existed or did not exist, but that organizations can demonstrate degrees of bureaucracy. Neither Weber nor Fayol use the formal organization as the point of departure in their discussion of organizing principles such as division of labor, hierarchy, specialization and written documentation. Although bureaucratic organizing in organization studies has become synonymous with the formal organization, it is not. It is merely a way of organizing – inside, outside or among formal organizations. The organizing principles I listed in Chapter 3 were:

- Responsibility
- Division of labor
- Specialization
- Hierarchical authority
- Centralization
- Coherence
- Impartiality
- Coordination
- Rational authority
- Rules for procedures and processes
- Documented processes
- Formalization
- Standardization

In the analysis model I stated that, if the control regime is to be understood as the organizing of and among organizations, one or more organizing principles should be used within the control regime. Based on my analysis, I am able to show that all of these organizing principles are used in the construction of the global control regime. There is the principle of responsibility explicitly being placed on the manufacturer. The organizations are controlled through a division of labor, specialization and a conceived hierarchy (Juxtaposition A). There are articulated descriptions of formalization and of standardization (through standards). There are arguments for coherence and clarity through the creation of a coherent unity (Juxtaposition D). There is centralization through creation of a hub: fewer organizations are to perform accreditation than are to perform certification. This is illustrated by a narrowing of the top of the triangle (Figure 5.4) (Juxtaposition C). In the control regime there are requirements for impartiality (the organizations must be independent and impartial). The hub creates coordination within the control regime. The control regime is characterized by a rational authority in the sense of a belief in rules. Both the control instruments and manuals for the control instruments are composed of various forms of rules for procedures (directives, standards, rules, guides, regulations and legislation) and link to each other and to the tools and objects of control in different ways (Juxtaposition B). The procedures apply in part to processes within organizations and in part to processes in the control regime. And finally, the instruments (standards) control by requiring documented routines and processes in the bodies controlled (organizations).

Bureaucracy means to 'control from one's desk' – stemming from its etymological roots of *bureau* (French: 'desk') and *kratein* (Greek: 'to govern or control') (Starbuck 2003) – in effect, controlling without direct contact between people. Perrow describes how 'factory bureaucracy replaced direct controls with rules and procedures' (Perrow 1991: 743). In other words, bureaucratic organizing principles are a way of controlling at a distance, where people don't need to be in direct contact with each other since written rules, routines and procedures replace such direct contact.

Control at a distance by way of bureaucratic organizing principles occurs in two ways. First, the written documentation that makes up bureaucratic organizing can be interpreted based on ideas about control at a distance, where all the written documentation that circulates constitutes a form of inscription, in Latour's terms (Latour 1987; Robson 1992). The bureaucratic organizing principles thereby enable control without direct contact between people, and control based on inscriptions that can be transferred from one place to another. Second, the control regime is organized according to the bureaucratic principles presented by Fayol (1916/2008), Weber (1922/1983), Hall (1963) and Perrow (1991). But in the control regime, they are principles for controlling organizations, not principles for controlling inside organizations. The bureaucratic organizing principles make control possible without the requirement that the control occur *within* an organization, which in turn enables control at greater distances than control that is limited to occurring only within an organization (even though some organizations are vastly spread out).

This line of reasoning also has consequences for how the formal organization can be interpreted in relation to control at a distance.

ORGANIZATIONS AS INTERCHANGEABLE, STANDARDIZED OBJECTS

As determined in Chapter 3, in the global control regime, the objects of control are organizations, not physical things. Seeing organizations as quasi-objects enabled me to include organizations in the analysis without making them theoretical units, such as 'formal organizations.' But the analysis of the global control regime also shows that the more standardized organizations become, the more interchangeable they become too. That organizations have become interchangeable, standardized objects is a development that has occurred during the emergence of the control regime. One could say that the standardization of organizations into interchangeable objects is *both the cause and the effect* of the global control regime.

CONTROL BY MEANS OF DOCUMENTATION OF ORGANIZATIONAL PROCESSES

When the Swedish national testing system was replaced by the Global Approach, the idea of self-conducted monitoring, where the manufacturer controls its own production process, was introduced. To do this, quality systems described in standards were used. Rather than inspecting physical products before they are released to the market, the manufacturer follows standards and documents the procedures of its manufacturing process in writing. Quality assurance and internal control emerged at the same time, in parallel. The quality assurance standard is an instrument that allows the EU to control the manufacturer. Through quality assurance and internal control, the EU got manufacturers to control themselves.

Controlling organizational processes by way of quality assurance came to apply to more controls than just manufacturers' internal control: a notified body's control of a manufacturer applies to the manufacturer's quality assurance system, and for a notified body to become accredited requires that the notified body also have a quality assurance system. An accreditation organization must in turn have a documented quality assurance system in order to operate within the Global Approach. With the introduction of the Goods Package, accreditation organizations were to be members of the EA, and to become a member they must be in compliance with the ISO 17011 standard, which stipulates that the accreditation organizations must have a documented quality assurance system. All of the controls in the modular system build on the quality assurance systems modeled in the ISO-9001 series.

In other words, as the control regime emerged, the focus of control was increasingly placed on organizational processes, rather than on control of physical products.

DOCUMENTED PROCESSES ARE PLACED IN ORGANIZATIONS

Several steps in the development of the control regime have meant that the written and documented organizational processes are placed and carried out within and directed at physical, legal and named places – namely, organizations.

First, the Goods Package (from 2008) requires that manufacturers, importers and distributors, accreditation bodies, notified bodies, notifying bodies, and market surveillance authorities are legal persons.

Second, the Goods Package also brought with it a requirement that the manufacturer give its address and ID number on the product, as well as the registered company name. Even the importer is required to give its address and registered name. If a notified body has inspected a manufacturer's production, the notified body's name must also be stated in the manufacturer's declaration.

Third, accreditation was defined in relation to another form of conformity assessment in that accreditation can only be carried out on a body that conducts conformity assessments – not on physical products. The object of accreditation must be a legal person with a name and an address, that is, an organization.

The standardization in the control regime has increasingly come to be directed at organizational processes rather than physical products. If I continue the analogy between the standardization of organizations and the standardization of physical things like nuts and bolts, the first step toward blurring the line between the controller and the controlled is now created – the controller (an organization) is the same as the controlled (an organization), as compared to when the controller (an organization) controls a physical thing (a nut or a bolt).

ORGANIZATIONS AS INTERCHANGEABLE TOOLS

In Chapter 3 I noted that from an action net perspective organizations have no core, there is no 'true nature' of the organization. Organizations can thereby be interpreted differently: as legal persons, as natural systems, or as actors. To understand how the control regime is able to get organizations to join a regime, I suggested that it was difficult to interpret organizations as independent, autonomous and sovereign actors, and I interpreted the formal organization instead as an artefact, a quasi-object (Czarniawska 2013).

In this control regime organizations are used to control at a distance; it is organizations that constitute the actual objects of control, at the same time as it is organizations that are the tools used to control. The purpose of the control is to standardize organizations. The standardization of organizations and the standardization of nuts and bolts are motivated in the same way: standardization of organizations makes organizations function more effectively because they can be coordinated, similarly to how a standard nut works effectively with a standard bolt because the two fit together. As opposed to standardization of nuts and bolts, however, standardization of organizations also facilitates further control of them. In the control regime, the standardization itself becomes a means of control. In other words, the purpose of the control (to standardize organizations) becomes the means, and the means (to standardize organizations) becomes the purpose.

The standardization of organizations creates the second step toward blurring the line between the controller and the controlled: because it is standardized organizations, and not nuts and bolts, that are being controlled, in the control regime there is essentially no difference between the standardized organizations that control and the standardized organizations that are controlled. A nut or a bolt itself cannot ensure that it follows a standard, but a formal organization can. This is most apparent in a manufacturer's internal control. It is also apparent in that most organizations are tasked with controlling others, at the same time as they themselves are controlled by still others. The objects of control are both controlled objects and controlling objects.

The analogy between standardization of nuts and bolts and standardization of organizations is a real analogy – organizations can also be mass-produced, consumed and discarded once they have filled their purpose (Czarniawska 2013). In the control regime, organizations become interchangeable tools. Interchangeability is created in several ways: the division of labor and specialization make the function itself the important point, not the one who performs it. Accreditation and certification can be performed by every body that fulfils the requirements. The work involved with mutual acceptance builds on the idea that things should be the same everywhere. All organizations that follow the same standard should all arrive at the same result. The idea that independent organizations should arrive at the same result also builds on the same result being achievable no matter who performs the activities, as long as they follow a standard.

DIFFERENT MEANINGS OF DISTANCE

In Chapter 3 I established that distance is a measure or estimation of the distance between two or more objects. Distance can be geometric and spatial when measured between two points. Distance can also be relational and temporal or cognitive (perceived distance). The components in the control regime are juxtaposed such that distance is bridged or eliminated. At the same time, in some cases these juxtapositions create the distance to be bridged or eliminated. Let me demonstrate how this is done.

First of all, the global control regime eliminates temporal distance. A product is CE-marked as evidence that the product complies with standards and directives. CE-marking is a snapshot that symbolizes the character of the product at the time of marking. In the global control regime, the CE mark also bridges forward in time into the future, however, from the time of marking to when a market surveillance authority sees it. The manufacturer, the importer and the distributor must ensure that the product maintains the same form, character, and characteristics as at the time of marking. CE-marking thus freezes time and eliminates the control regime's temporal distance – the CE mark communicates from the past (when the control was performed), via the present (when someone sees the mark), into the future (the CE mark is to withstand time and remain valid).

Second, in that the manufacturer, the importer and the distributor are tasked with controlling one another, geometric distance is also bridged. The manufacturer must affix the CE mark and the importer must control that the manufacturer has affixed the CE mark, and the distributor must control that the importer has controlled that the manufacturer has affixed the CE mark. This creates a chain that interlinks the objects of control and bridges geometric distance since the importer, the distributor and the manufacturer are in different places in relation to one another (Juxtaposition B). Even the work of the IAF to make accredited certifications apply throughout the world has to do with geometric distance: it doesn't matter where a certification was performed, as long as the certification organization is accredited it applies and is 'accepted everywhere.'

In some cases, the control regime creates distance by the same means by which it aims to bridge distance. The control regime creates relational distance through a specific division of labor (Juxtaposition A); creating what is referred to in the field material as 'different levels.' The control regime is organized as a hierarchy. The division of labor is to keep the certification organizations, accreditation organizations, market surveillance organizations, manufacturers, importers and distributors independent from each other. Independence and the hierarchy serve to create distance between the different organizations – one way of interpreting the ongoing work within the control regime to have the participating organizations 'independent' from one another is that 'independence' is all about keeping a distance. But at the same time, the global control regime is meant to link accreditation and certification organizations all across the world, which is achieved partly by the chain-like linkages between the organizations (Juxtaposition B) and partly by the same division of labor of the components that arranges them in the hierarchy (Juxtaposition A). The division of labor and chain-like connection holds the organizations in constant contact with each other, a requirement for the control regime to exist. In other words, the control regime creates a hierarchical distance between organizations *at the same time* as the organizations are placed in relation to one another by the same hierarchy.

In Law's model from 1986, the assumption of distance rests on the fact that the controller is assumed to be at a distance from the controlled. Control at a distance builds in turn on a notion of distance between the controller and the controlled that requires certain methods for making control possible. For Law, this had to do with being able to control ships at a distance, when the controllers were no longer in contact with the controlled – they couldn't hear, see or talk to each other, or in other ways have direct contact. The geometric distance in Law's seafaring case was able to be bridged by means of trained seamen, well-equipped ships, and a written and simplified interpretation of navigation systems.

Things are different in the global control regime. In the global control regime the separation between the controller and the controlled disappears – the controller and the controlled are in many cases the same objects, and both the controller and the controlled are standardized. There are two consequences to this: that the distance becomes *absorbed* by the control regime, and that control is created *without anybody having absolute control*.

STANDARDS AND ABSORPTION OF DISTANCE

Perrow (1991) wrote that organizations absorb society. The control regime, made up of a multitude of standardized, controlling and controlled organizations, absorbs distance. In the global control regime this distance is organized *into* the control regime, as a part of its construction.

The absorbing of distance has to do with standards. In contrast to control that was founded on a geometric distance between the controller (the principal) and the controlled (the agent) (Law 1986), standards are ubiquitous, they are everywhere and can be most closely likened to the skies used by the Portuguese in Law's study to create navigation systems. Standards are used and control in many contexts, in many places, and by and within many organizations at the same time. Standards constitute a 'strong explanation' (Robson 1992) and eliminate, by their ever-presence, the distance between the controller and the controlled.

Timmermans and Epstein write that standards are 'phenomena that help regulate and calibrate social life by rendering the modern world equivalent across cultures, time and geography' (Timmermans and Epstein 2010: 70), and that is precisely how the global control regime works – standards calibrate both time and geometry, allowing the meaning of time and geometry to be absorbed as aspects of distance: the control regime has built in, incorporated and absorbed time, geography and relations between objects.

In Law's control regime, ships were sent off and later returned. The possibility of coming back is central and in turn creates the need for control that makes mobility, stability and permanency possible (so that what is sent out is able to return). In the control regime, it is standards that – like drones – move across time and space while the organizations controlled remain in place, or symbolically shift. Standards are to monitor and carry information within a set area or territory – the clear division of labor of the ISO 17011 standard for accreditation, ISO 17021 standard for certification and ISO 9001 for quality assurance (Juxtaposition A) create the boundaries that define the area within which the respective drone/standard should stay. The likening of standards to drones also illustrates the likeness between the control regime and Law's conclusion that in order for the control to work the components must return. To remain current and effective, every now and then drones must return to their place of origin, that is, a standard must return to the ISO to be revised or reconnected to EU directives.

To summarize, the creation and elimination of distance in the control regime differ from how distance is discussed in earlier texts on control at a distance. In Law's model distance is geometric. The control occurred from a distance: from Portugal to other parts of the world. It was also physical: ships were to sail from one place to another. Even Robson (1992) treats distance as something physical. In Law's model distance is absolute. In the global control regime distance is relative – relational and hierarchical, temporal, or spatial (Sundström 2011; Corvellec, Ek, Zapata and Zapata Campos 2016). Control at a distance in the global control regime is made possible by absorbing temporal and geometric distance, by distance becoming a part of the global control regime. The spatial aspect is still there, but is built into the global control regime rather than something to be bridged or eliminated. Spatially distant organizations are now part of the same unity – the control regime.

CONTROL WITHOUT ANYBODY CONTROLLING?

> Texts of all sorts, machines or other physical objects, and people, sometimes separately but more frequently in combination, these seem to be the obvious raw materials for the *actor* who seeks to control others at a distance. (Law 1986: 255, emphasis added)

In Law's passage the Portuguese are the controlling actors. The components are passive agents. Passive agents presuppose a principal – some body that controls the agent ('the actor who seeks to control others at a distance'). In the global control regime I have analysed, there is no body corresponding to the Portuguese – there is no principal.

In the control regime standards are the foundation but the standardization organizations that publish standards are not principals because a standard presupposes an organization that ensures that it is followed, which the manufacturer itself, the certification organizations, the accreditation organizations or the EA does. This also means that none of the organizations that create control instruments in the regime can be seen as the sole controller, the principal. The EU and the national governments create manuals for how the control instruments (standards) are to be used; their control is not absolute or exclusive.

The accreditation organizations are made coordinating hubs (Juxtaposition C) and given a specific role, but the accreditation organizations are not only controllers, they are also controlled. Because the control regime is constructed like a chain (Juxtaposition B), the organizations are connected to another organization that controls the next organization in the chain. The accreditation organizations are not the sole controller because they are themselves controlled by the EA. The EA is not the sole controller because the EA is controlled by the EU. Neither does the EU have absolute control because the regime reaches beyond the Union's borders, by way of IAF agreements. The IAF is not the sole controller since its actions are based on operations run by the EA (or other regional equivalents around the world). And the EA gets its mandate from the EU.

Because there is no real difference between the controlling and the controlled organizations in the control regime, the global control regime is made up of a collective of controlled organizations that control each other, without any one body being absolute controller. In the control regime there is no principal, only agents, or every body is a principal and an agent at the same time.

Neither does the control regime have a center. There are centralization processes in which a smaller number of organizations are to perform accreditation than the number of organizations that are to perform certification, though the coordinating hubs are not to be regarded as centers, but simply as hubs that are standardized and controlled. And without a center, there is no periphery. The periphery is incorporated into the regime by the different ways in which the control regime incorporates its environment. Without a center and without a periphery the control regime differs from Law's case, where center and periphery are in contact. In the control regime, there is unbroken communication without a center and periphery being in contact.

It also becomes clear that, when compared to Law's control model, the control regime is missing one type of component: people. The control regime is built by people but is aimed at organizations and documents, not people. This can be likened to how the ideal bureaucratic model assigns bureaucrats (people) a neutral and impartial role. In the global control regime it is instead the objects of control that are standardized to become impartial and independent. The control regime becomes a bureaucracy populated by organizations.

To sum up, in the global control regime I studied, there is a division of labor, there are coordinating hubs, and there are links between the organizations. And even if the regime is made up of organizations separated from one another, the control (including self-conducted monitoring) forms a coherent whole: the control regime.

In some respects this description of the control regime is consistent with the theoretical ideas that explain control at a distance. There is unbroken communication in the control regime, and the control regime has incorporated its environment. But there are also interesting differences between the global control regime and other types of control at a distance. In the control regime, bureaucratic principles are used for the control *of* organizations, not *within* them. And the control regime does not have an equivalent to a controlling principal (in Law's case, the Portuguese). In this control regime organizations are both agents and objects upon which the agents act. In this control regime there is no central decision-maker, no king, no boss, no captain. The control regime is made up of a number of controlled organizations with no one body that controls all the rest. In contrast to Law's idea that assumes an objectively existing geometric distance, in the control regime there is relational and hier-archic distance, and temporal and spatial distance, both of which are created and absorbed by the control regime's own organizing. This is how the control is made possible.

8. The control regime, the state and responsibility

I began this book by asking how we are able to trust products and organizations in our global world. This then led me to ask how a global control regime was constructed. I also asked about what components were used to build the global control regime and how these components fit together. Then I asked more specifically about accreditation and what role it might play in the construction of the global control regime. It is now time to answer these questions and consider the answers in relation to earlier research.

My point of departure was that standardization, certification and accreditation are activities that constitute a complex order and it is this order that I seek to understand. My starting point was therefore that these activities are linked to each other and that how they link together makes control possible, and I wondered how and why this is so. In Chapter 1 I also introduced the concept of a *control regime* in order to discuss the interconnectedness of standards, certification and accreditation. A control regime is an order that controls. The concept of *regime* has been used earlier in the standardization and certification research (Loconto and Busch 2010; Hatanaka, Konefal and Constance 2012; Fouilleux and Loconto 2016) for descriptive purposes without theoretical or analytical meaning.

In order to answer the questions about the construction of the control regime, I turned to earlier research on standards, certification and accreditation. But earlier research has in part had a sectoral focus (studies that examined standardization and certification. in agriculture and forestry, for example), and in part described standards and certification as something governed by private law and driven by the market. I also noted a lack of research on the role of accreditation in relation to standardization and certification. Because accreditation is not included in earlier studies, there are both analytical and empirical limitations in the studies that have attempted to look at how standards and certification together construct a global control regime.

THE COMPONENTS OF THE CONTROL REGIME AND THEIR JUXTAPOSITION

Working on theories of control at a distance, in Chapter 3 I presented three ideas of how the components should be positioned in relation to each other in order to make control possible. I called this relation their 'juxtaposition.' Juxtaposition, I wrote, refers to more than position or relation; juxtaposition is where the two components combined create something that they do not create on their own.

In Chapter 6, I analysed my field material and answered the question of what components were used to build the control regime: the bodies that create the control instruments in the control regime, namely, the standards organizations ISO and CEN. The control regime is constructed with the control instruments of standards, and manuals for these standards in the form of legislation, guides, directives, regulations and resolutions. The control regime is built with tools to control – in part different forms of instruments, and in part organizations as tools to control. Finally, in addition to these components, the control regime is constructed with that which is to be controlled – organizations. Organizations are the control regime's objects of control. In other words, organizations are both tools used to control and the objects to be controlled.

To summarize, these components are juxtaposed in such a way as to create a division of labor in the control regime and in chain-like organizing. How the components are juxtaposed also leads to the creation of a hub in the regime, and an idea of a coherent unity. Together the four components and their juxtapositions make control at a distance possible in the control regime, which is thereby able to become global.

A critical part of the global control regime is the control instrument – standards. Standards are what form the foundation for everything else. Without standards the control regime would not exist, though with only standards it would not be able to operate either. If standards had been only standards and not been linked to certification, or if certification had not been linked to accreditation, the control regime would not have been able to become controlling. It is once the components are assembled in the way I have shown that the control regime is able to control and become global.

The control regime has absorbed the distance it was to control. Organizations are no longer distant from each other but a part of the same whole, the same control regime. The spatial aspect of distance is still there – there is still a spatial distance between one organization and other organizations in the control regime. But the relational, temporal and cognitive distance is absorbed – no matter where organizations operate they follow the same standards and the same certifications. The glocality discussed by Robertson (1992) or the practical and material aspects of globalization underlined by Law and Mol (2008) are also visible in the control regime. By following the same standard – the same PDF file – the control regime becomes both global and local at the same time. The control regime is global in construction but its activities are local. So – rather than calling it global – the control regime should perhaps instead be called 'glocal.'

THE ROLE OF ACCREDITATION IN A GLOBAL CONTROL REGIME

The second sub-question posed in the book is a more practically oriented one because I wondered what role accreditation plays in a global control regime. Earlier research on standards, certification and accreditation uses a number of different concepts to indicate the voluntary and market-driven aspects of standards and certification. As I pointed out in Chapter 1, a piece of the puzzle is missing in these descriptions: accreditation.

The answer to the question of the role of accreditation in a global control regime is that accreditation works as a coordinating hub. Accreditation was the link from the national testing system to the EU's Global Approach. When the national testing system was decommissioned, the part of the system that worked with authorization was maintained, authorization became accreditation, and the former National Council for Metrology and Testing became the national accreditation organization Swedac. Swedac thus became, as did its equivalents around the world, a hub for certification and standards.

I have shown how accreditation is distinguished from certification, especially because accreditation activities are linked to organizations with public authority status. This is in contrast to certification, which is not to be conducted by public organizations. At the same time as accreditation is made a specific hub in the control regime, accreditation is a component in a larger order. Accreditation – together with the ISO standards for quality assurance, certification, the modules, the principle of presumption, MLA agreements, membership, self-conducted monitoring, manufacturers, importers, distributors, market surveillance authorities, notifying bodies, notified bodies and CE-marking – creates the control regime. The answer to the question of what role accreditation plays in a global control regime must therefore be understood in the context of the other components of the control regime, and the answer to the first sub-question, presented above. The analysis of the control regime also shows that the answer to the book's first sub-question could not have been arrived at if I had not studied accreditation specifically. The study of the development from a national testing system, via the Global Approach and the Goods Package, to World Accreditation Day shows that accreditation is a function embedded in a larger order. An important and critical function, but not an isolated one.

FINDINGS IN RELATION TO EARLIER RESEARCH

The answers to the questions posed above entail some adjustment to conclusions drawn in earlier studies of the organizing of standards and certification. Earlier research on standardization and certification has analysed the organizing of these activities as something 'non-state market-based' or a form of 'hybrid fields of governance,' as arisen out of a 'policy void' and a form of self-regulation that has emerged in sectors where the state does not want, is unable, or is not permitted to regulate and control. An analysis of the control regime paints a somewhat different picture.

The control regime builds on an idea where commercial certification companies compete with one another. A market for certification is thereby created in and with the control regime. The Global Approach, the Goods Package and the IAF can to a certain extent be traced back to attempts to create a European and, later, global market for products and services. Earlier research has presented certification as market-based, as private-law initiatives created either in the absence of state regulation or as having arisen out of market forces where consumer demand for controlled and regulated products generates standardization and certification (Bernstein and Cashore 2007; Bartley 2011; Marx 2008; Hatanaka, Konefal and Constance 2012). But the organizing of the control regime is in itself not market-based – the parts that make up the control regime (accreditation, certification, MLA agreements, control based on standards, the principle of presumption, the modular system, market surveillance, division of economic operators and notified bodies) cannot be explained as primarily commercially driven market orders. Most of the organizations that are the components of the control regime are certainly companies that operate in markets (e.g. different product markets or markets for certification), but the organizing of the control regime does not have to do with creating markets, but rather with controlling organizations and absorbing distance. It is difficult to see how the complex organization constituted by the control regime could be called a 'market' (Brunsson and Jutterström 2018).

Closely linked to explaining certification as something driven by market and commercial forces, are ideas of how standardization and certification have arisen out of a policy void where states are unable or not permitted to regulate (Bernstein and Cashore 2007). Even concepts like *emerging* (see Bartley 2011) serve to describe certification as something that has developed incrementally, without having been driven by a state or clearly articulated decisions. Yet the control regime I studied is built on directives, laws, regulations, rules, standards and resolutions. For the 40 years it has been developing, the control regime has been built on various explicit policies. The control regime is decided, traceable and formalized – the opposite of something incrementally arisen without decisions or an identifiable dispatcher in a void or in a market.

In relation to emphasizing the market and commercial drivers behind the growth of certification, the research has also stressed that certification is carried out as a non-state control – it is as a private form of control that certification distinguishes itself and gains legitimacy (Bernstein and Cashore 2007). Even though the fact that standardization and certification are created and carried out in relation to public organizations and public-law rules has been pointed out – 'certification systems are more intertwined with states and less straightforward in their effects than many previous discussions imply' (Bartley 2011: 441) – the role of the state has been mentioned more in passing or as a detail for future research to study. Studies on standards and certification have been done on both companies and associations, but seldom on public authorities. The control regime I studied provides a clear picture of the state's role in relation to standardization, certification and accreditation that earlier research has not shown. Sweden's national testing sites were to be state-operated to guarantee independent control. Some 30 years later, the control is again state-run to guarantee independence, not through national testing sites, but through accreditation. The Goods Package meant that the accreditation organizations throughout the EU, were to be given public authority status, were to be non-commercial, and were not to compete with each other, all for the purpose of creating trust and guaranteeing independent control. Considering the important function accreditation fills – and the role the state plays via accreditation in the control regime – it is altogether misleading to refer to the control regime as 'non-state.' The state has served and continues to serve an increasingly important function in the organizing of the control regime throughout its development.

During the control regime's 40 years of development, boundaries and roles between companies and authorities, private-law and public-law, have been strengthened. Under the national testing system no substantive distinction was made between whether a control was governed by an official regulation or a standard, or whether certification was performed by a public authority or a company. Frankel and Hojbjerg (2007) show that private-law standardizers are able to perform political tasks, but this does not mean that the boundaries are blurred or the roles are hybrid. Certification has been described as creating transnational 'hybrid fields of governance' (Bartley 2011) due to the entwining of state and private regulation that certification and standardization represents. It has similarly been claimed that the distinction between the roles of private and public organizations is, by way of standards, certification and accreditation, slowly disappearing (Fouilleux and Loconto 2016). I have shown that the regime is organized through specialization and division of labor between organizations that has become clearer and clearer over time. The roles were less distinct and more entwined in the 1980s than they are 30 years later; rather, the roles have gone from being hybrid to being more distinct. That the control regime is composed of both state and private organizations does not mean their roles are entwined; they are instead clearly articulated and designed precisely to create a distinction between private and public, not to erase the boundary.

The concept of self-regulation has also been used to describe the market- and commercially oriented nature of standardization and certification. Self-regulation can mean either that industries themselves create the rules that companies follow (Haufler 2003, Meyer and Bromley 2013) or self-regulation can mean that the market creates 'name and shame' mechanisms that, with no involvement of state organizations or mandatory rules, determine which companies remain in the market and which don't (Bartley 2011). The control regime is made up of organizations that govern and control other organiza- tions. The rules that control the organizations – standards – come from the EU or ISO. The rules do not come from the standard-following organizations themselves, nor have the rules grown out of abstract market mechanisms. The whole point of the control regime's division of labor and specialization is for different activities – such as rule-setting – to be handled by organizations other than those that use the rules. This is one of the reasons why the control regime is composed of so many organizations. To call the control regime 'self-regulating' would therefore not be appropriate.

The control regime is more complex, more well-organized, reaches across more organizations and more countries than earlier research has shown. Below, I discuss four aspects of the control regime that, given my analysis and findings, can be problematized, and that earlier research has not focused on.

CENTER AND PERIPHERY IN THE CONTROL REGIME

In the control regime the boundary between who controls and who is con- trolled is erased, which I stated in Chapter 7. Organizations are both tools that control and objects that are controlled. In other words, an organization can be both controller and controlled at the same time. The ubiquitously present standardization by means of standards makes the control regime's way of con- trolling at a distance different from explanations of control at a distance given in the earlier literature: there, there was a principal who controlled the agent. By the control regime's rubbing out of the boundary between controllers and the controlled, the principal becomes agent and the agent principal. The control regime has no center and therefore no periphery either, which I also noted in Chapter 7.

The control regime's organizing for ubiquitous control (in that every body controls an other body, including itself) could be likened to Foucault's

(1975/1987) *panopticon* – control of many at the same time. The idea of a panopticon is based on the existence of a central place from which the control can be performed. In the control regime, however, no such equivalent exists, neither physically nor metaphorically. The likening of standards to hovering drones deployed in a division of labor makes the control regime resemble more Latour's (2005) *oligopticon* – where everyone sees a little bit but no-one sees the whole: 'From oligoptica, sturdy but extremely narrow views of the (connected) whole are made possible' (Latour 2005: 181). All of the organizations in the control regime control some body while no-one controls every body. In this way control is created in the control regime, without a central controlling principal or panopticon.

RESPONSIBILITY IN THE CONTROL REGIME

Because there is no center and no one body that controls the control regime, responsibility becomes a problem. Organizations can be interpreted as legal persons and as such, they can be ascribed responsibility (Lamoreaux 2004), from a purely legal standpoint at least. Every organization in the control regime thereby is a carrier of its own responsibility, in a legal sense. This means that it is difficult, in a control regime built on so many standardized organizations, to attach responsibility to a specific organization, even more so when the organization in question is mass-produced, interchangeable, standardized and consumable (according to the analogy of organizations and physical things).

Since the time of Fayol (1916/2008), it has been taken for granted that responsibility is hierarchically organized. In the control regime there is hierarchical organizing because the different activities are described as being situated at different levels in relation to one another, where accreditation is a level above certification, and where the organization 'on top' of the other is entitled to make decisions and control the one 'under' it. The control regime has even been depicted as a pyramid, a classic way of illustrating organiza-tional organizational hierarchy (though see also Ohlsson and Rombach 1998). But in contrast to hierarchical organizations where hierarchy is linked to leadership figures in a position and with the authority to control the organiza-tion vertically, the control regime has no such equivalent. There is no CEO, no director-general, and no secretary-general. And thereby there is no central or absolute leader in charge – the manufacturer is responsible for its product and for following the rules required for internal control, but is not responsible for the rules created or the content of the control itself. The standardization organizations create standards but are not responsible for implementing the standards, or their ensuing consequences. Certification companies are respon-sible for certification but not for the standard that determines how certification should be carried out and not for the certified manufacturer. Accreditation organizations are responsible for accreditation but not for certification, and so on. There is no collective responsibility for the control regime as a whole: every body is responsible for its link in the chain, but no one body for the entire chain.

Another aspect that makes responsibility in the control regime problematic is the characteristics assigned to standards. In legal settings where rules are mandatory to follow, the responsibility of what the rule causes are generally with the rule setter such as parliaments or other legislative organizations. For standards, it is different. Compliance with the standards that make up the entire foundation of the control regime is voluntary, which makes accountability difficult (Brunsson and Jacobsson 2000) – is it the standardization organization that is responsible for standards or the body that chooses to follow them? Because of specific decisions in the control regime, the standardization organizations are responsible only for writing the standards, not for what happens when they are implemented. Here, the clear division of labor between the components has a diffusing effect on responsibility. The problem of responsibility becomes even more serious in cases where standards are used to control public authorities. When a standard is used to control authorities, the government's ability to influence the rule that controls its authority is very limited – the government did not create the standard, ISO did. This means that the government cannot be held accountable either, for what the standard stipulates.

THE STATE'S ROLE IN THE CONTROL REGIME

The control regime has consequences for the role of the state in a globalized world. Earlier research has shown that the state's role in Europeanization is rule-driven, fragmented and intertwined (Jacobsson, Pierre and Sundström 2015).

Going back to the example of Sweden, the Swedish government creates manuals, not control instruments. The Swedish accreditation organization and state authority Swedac is controlled by an ISO standard. ISO 17011 is the instrument used to control the authority. In the control regime other forms of control instruments that the government normally has access to, in order to control its authorities, such as government appropriations and instructions, are to be viewed more as manuals for the standard – government directives and instructions only reaffirm and refer to the content of the standard. Swedac becomes an 'ISO-ified' authority, its main purpose is to control others with standards, as well as being controlled itself by standards. In Chapter 2 I described the characteristics of standards and one of these was that standards are not created in national parliaments but in ISO committees. This means that the government controls neither the control regime nor the control regime's national hub. This has severe consequences for democratic control: the use of standards in the control of public authorities breaks the democratic chain of command in which the government bears the responsibility for controlling state activities.

At the same time, and somewhat contradictorily, great efforts have been made to make accreditation into something with public authority status (e.g. by using crowns in the logo). It would appear important that there be, within the control regime, a state function, a representative tasked with creating trust precisely by its connection to the state and its authority status. An interesting contradiction arises here – the state function that is to yield the control regime trust through its 'stateliness,' is highly 'ISO-ified' and controlled by rules that the state has not created and cannot be responsible for.

Viewed over the course of the control regime's 40-year development, the testing and control system has gone from being a completely state-controlled order to an order where companies control themselves. From an order where Swedish parliament and government determined, via the public authorities, what was to be regulated in products, to an order where this is decided in the committees of standardization organizations. This has been argued for clearly and explicitly over the course of the control regime's emergence – authorities were not to serve as *ex ante* controllers and the control regime was not to become a sluggish, bureaucratic machine.

THE CONTROL REGIME AS SOMETHING UNPOLITICAL

The changed roles of the state and companies that I describe can be seen as a part of a larger development of public sector organizing, often referred to as new public management (NPM). But, as opposed to the privatization of many other sectors like education, health care and elderly care, telecom networks, railways or postal services, the privatization of state testing and control has taken place under the political radar. Consumers and citizens are not always aware of what the CE mark stands for or the role the state plays in product safety, because the CE mark is not directed towards the public but a signal from one organization in the control regime, to another.

The control regime's development has occurred in silence but it hasn't been shaded or hidden from view. Quite the opposite – the largest part of the field material has comprised public records, and various political decisions along the way have created space for the control regime. The lack of attention surrounding the organizing of control may have to do with its technical nature: both the research on standards and practitioners in the control regime indicate that standards often go unnoticed (Timmermans and Epstein 2010) or, as expressed in one of my interviews, that 'accreditation is perhaps not the sexiest topic of discussion.' The terminology used in the control regime also makes it difficult to gain entry to and an understanding and overview of how it works. The control regime with its many parts quite simply has a hard time reaching out, presenting itself as politically significant and interesting to the media, despite its immense influence all around the world. And if people don't know about it, they cannot change it or question it. The global control regime therefore can keep expanding, without resistance.

BUREAUCRACY THROUGH NON-BUREAUCRATIZATION

The control has another connection the idea of the state – the control regime has become a bureaucracy. The concept of bureaucracy can be used in different ways. It can be used, as I have used it in the analysis of the control regime, as an analytical concept to understand a certain kind of organizing according to certain principles, an interpretation in line with Hall (1963), for example. Weber's model of ideal-typical bureaucracy was not placed in the formal organization as an entity but was made up of principles for organizing public administration. Using such an interpretation, the control regime resembles a bureaucracy – it is, after all, constructed like one.

'Bureaucracy' can also be understood as a single entity – *one* bureaucracy. In this case the word is often used synonymously with public administration and can be seen both as an instrument and as an institution (Olsen 2003). In interpretations of bureaucracy as an instrument, the point of departure is that bureaucracy is a means for achieving something else, usually a political agenda. Bureaucracy implements the policy in a neutral, objective and efficient manner. The bureaucracy thereby becomes the agent and the politicians become the principal. As agent and instrument, bureaucracy has no sovereignty, no autonomy, no identity (Bromley and Meyer 2015), a bureaucracy cannot decide, that is done by its 'head.'

It is the instrument kind of bureaucracy that is often criticized. Its officials either follow the bureaucratic ideal too faithfully or work for their own gain – two critical arguments against the bureaucracy that, according to du Gay (2000), cancel each other out. The criticism of bureaucracy often has to do with its rigid construction, a construction that is seen as both immoral (it doesn't take the individual's personal needs and circumstances into consideration) and ineffective (Crozier 1964).

Bureaucracy can also be understood as an institution with its own norms and values (Olsen 2003). Du Gay (2000) defends bureaucracy as an organizational form by claiming, based on Weber, that bureaucracy has been unfairly judged against an ethos founded on values other than those the bureaucracy is meant to protect. A bureaucracy is not meant to protect people's existential freedom and can therefore not be held responsible when it does not. A bureaucracy constitutes its own ethos, its own moral domain, and can only be evaluated based on the premises on which it operates – as a means for rationally implementing the tasks assigned to it by its principal (du Gay 2000; Olsen 2003). Another line of defense was given by Perrow (1986), who wrote that the reason for the ineffectiveness of organizations is due not to over-bureaucratization but rather to under-bureaucratization. An organization that is completely bureaucratized – a state that can hardly be achieved since Weber's bureaucracy was an ideal type – is also by far the most effective organizational form to exist.

Most arguments for the creation of the control regime had to do with *not* creating a bureaucracy. The reasoning stemmed from criticism of the type summarized by du Gay: bureaucracies were regarded as something negative, something to be avoided – earlier orders were called rigid, ineffective and out-dated, and therefore the control regime was to be the opposite. And the control regime did not become a bureaucracy in the sense of a public administration. But in other ways it is a full-fledged bureaucratic order; all of the bureaucratic organizing principles can be found in the control regime. As an organizational model and as an instrument for implementing something, the control regime resembles a bureaucracy. In other words, the control regime came to be organized as a bureaucracy using the reasoning that it was precisely that which it was not to become, an interesting paradox. Maybe Weber was right after all. Maybe bureaucracy is the organizational form that ultimately takes over and is invincible.

The big and key difference between the control regime as a bureaucracy and public administration as a bureaucracy is that, from an ideal-typical standpoint, public administration relies on the law-governed state with articulated principles for accountability, the rule of law, and democracy – it is on these grounds it is defended and it is on these grounds it is able to constitute its own moral domain or institution (du Gay 2000; Olsen 2003). But accountability, the rule of law and democracy are fundamental values missing in the control regime. There is no principal that bears the responsibility and does the controlling. Neither can we vote on how the control regime is designed or hold its standards accountable in a court of law as we can with national law. Here again, the control regime has all of the attributes but none of the obligations.

9. Macro-organization

By now, it is time to substantiate the main theoretical argument of the book and to relate what I have been discussing so far, to the ongoing discussion in organization theory regarding how organization and organizing among organizations can be analysed and theorized. In doing so, I use the concept of *macro-organization* to understand and discuss, from a theoretical standpoint, the control regime as an organizational phenomenon.

At the end of the chapter, I connect back to the introduction of the book and talk about possible ways of understanding who an 'other' is and who we – as consumers, citizens and just ordinary people – become if the 'other' is a faceless, globe-spanning organization of organizations that cannot be closed down, declared insolvent or voted out.

THE CONTROL REGIME – AN ORGANIZATIONAL PHENOMENON

The main question of this book has had to do with understanding how a control regime built of organizations has been constructed – how is it made possible to have millions of organizations all over the world, organized into one regime? I have shown empirically what makes this possible, but the answer to the question also has a theoretical meaning. How does one, from an organization theory standpoint, understand the dense form of organizing that the control regime is built on? How can we understand the organizational phenomenon that arises when large numbers of organizations and a continuously ongoing organizing of these organizations are linked together to create a kind of coherent whole?

In the beginning of the book, I wrote that organization research had become locked into viewing the organization as an analytical and theoretical entity and thus studied that which is found 'outside' or among organizations as something else, as fields, as the surrounding environment, or as markets. My starting point was instead what I called the 'symmetrical perspective' of organization – that organization is not an order reserved for formal organizations, but an order than can be found both within and outside such envisioned entities. This makes the boundary between organization and environment as a starting point if not irrelevant at least of limited analytical importance. The control regime is at the same time largely built on the idea that organizations do exist and many of the activities that standardizers, certifiers and accreditors engage in are aimed at the notion of the formal organization. It seems that the formal organization is the only form of population that possesses citizenship in the control regime – people are secondary. Therefore, as I asked about the construction of the control regime, I needed to be able to create an understanding of formal organizations. In Chapters 3 and 7, I drew an analogy between organizations and physical things like nuts and bolts, and thereby also likened organizations to tools whose purpose was to build or create something (Perrow 1991; Czarniawska 2013). It is a fitting analogy because it elucidates the organizations as components of a larger whole. And, as components of a larger whole, organizations become interchangeable. A hammer fills a specific function and cannot be replaced by a screwdriver, but you do not need a specific hammer to hit a nail – only a tool of the hammer sort. Similarly, organizations are needed for the regime to function, but it does not have to be a specific organization. The organizations in the regime are standardized. Precisely like nuts and bolts, the organizations must be made similar so that they will fit in different places around the world. An accredited certification organization must be able to work everywhere where that accreditation is accepted: the activities performed in the regime are to be unambiguous and comparable – and interchangeable.

Viewing organizations as interchangeable tools also shows the difference this makes to how organizations are interpreted. In Chapter 3 I wrote that I interpreted organizations as quasi-objects. The analogy between standardization of physical things and standardization of organizations makes the meaning of the formal organization in the control regime different than in earlier research on standards and standardization, where the organization was the actual unit of analysis and the organization's behavior the analytical focus (e.g. Walgenbach 2001; Beck and Walgenbach 2005; Mendel 2006; Boiral 2012; Sandholtz 2012).

Viewing organizations as interchangeable tools helps to explain why the control regime has not become dependent on a specific organization. The control regime is not threatened if one certification company goes bankrupt or if one accreditation organization is replaced by another – it is the function that is important, not the specific organization.

There are several consequences to this way of understanding organizations. In Chapter 3 I also wrote that all of the principles – of the division of labor, coordination, specialization, centralization, formalization and standardization – presented in the research as principles to describe the internal order of organizations, can just as easily describe orders outside organizations. In this way the dichotomy between what is inside and what is outside an organization begins to disappear – orders outside as well as within organizations can be understood as organized. I turned the idea of the formal organization as a unit inside-out – that which is assumed to exist within an organization can also be found outside it. That was a first step in the analysis to theoretically understand the control regime. Now, I will turn it back again. What happens when all of the organization principles and all of the organizations are put together into a larger organizational phenomenon? What is the sum of all the parts? In order to understand how the control regime is composed as an organizational phenomenon, I discuss in the following sections a number of organization theory concepts that in different ways seek to capture and explain the increasing organization of society – both inside and among organizations.

THE CONTROL REGIME AND PARTIAL ORGANIZATION

Partial organization has emerged as a discussion in organization theory stemming from a 2011 article by Ahrne and Brunsson. The idea of partial organization follows the symmetrical perspective and builds on an idea that organization is based on decisions. Unlike other social orders such as networks or institutions that are non-decided and emergent, organization is a decided, social order. As mentioned, they presented five elements that are constitutive for formal organizations – rules, sanctions, membership, control and hierarchy. Ahrne and Brunsson argued that these elements can all be used as a framework for analysis to understand order both within, outside and among organizations. Organizations organize other organizations by deciding on rules for others to follow (such as standards), membership (organizations becoming members in other organizations) or sanctions (such as rankings or certifications). Today, there are a number of empirical studies that have used the five elements of organization as an analytical framework for understanding an increasing or decreasing level of organization as well as a combination of various elements in various contexts (see Ahrne and Brunsson 2019).

Partial organization can be viewed as a contribution to the theoretical debate to understand organizing among organizations. *Partial* organization means organized in parts or partially organized, which is why the entire conceptual structure implies a kind of diffusion of organization – that organization is not at all a composite packaged structure within the framework of the formal organization. Through its elements, organization can be understood as dispersed, partial. There can be a little organization or there can be a lot.

All of the five elements can be identified in the control regime. There are rules (standards, directives, laws, regulations, guiding documents), there are sanctions (unapproved certification, penalties for falsely claiming to be accredited by Swedac or other appointed accreditors), there is membership in the regional member organizations and the international member organization for accreditation, there is a hierarchy between the different organizations in who gets to decide over who, and there is, not least, control by way of certification, accreditation, market surveillance and peer review. The control regime can easily be understood as partially organized.

But what happens when all of the 'parts' in 'partial' organization are brought together? What happens when all elements are brought together into a single whole, into something 'complete' rather than 'partial'? In the framework of partial organization there are still no obvious analyses or concepts for this, which is why some important questions concerning the organizing among organizations still await answers.

Partial organization and the idea of understanding organization as a decided order both within, among and outside organizations is an important component in the symmetrical perspective. But partial organization stops right there, at 'partial,' and has yet to explain the sum of the parts.

THE CONTROL REGIME AND HYPER-ORGANIZATION

In 2015, Patricia Bromley and John W. Meyer introduced the concept of *hyper-organization* as a means of characterizing the ever-increasing organizing of society. It is rooted in a new institutional argument – that an increasing number of social orders are taking the form of a formal organization. Orders that could earlier be characterized as movements, tribes, groups or associations now have procedures and structures for accounting, decision-making and attaining goals. They have names, logos and slogans. Bromley and Meyer explain this increase of formal organizations as an expression of the rational institutional environment where, above all, a belief in science is prompting social orders to look and act in certain ways. In a 'world society' (Meyer 2010) these rational units have become universal – formal organizations are found all around the world and their structures are strikingly similar. The form for formal organization does not stop at the national border. 'Hyper,' in this context, illustrates the idea that a majority of these organizations are tasked with organizing other organizations, rather than producing physical things. Management consultants, accounting firms and PR agencies are some of many examples of organizations that make a living off of organizing others in continuously ongoing organization – hyper-organization. Meyer characterizes these organizations as 'others' (Meyer 2010).

The control regime could be described as a hyper-version of hyper-organization. The control regime can be regarded as a set of 'others' that is both organized and organizes others, the control regime is built by 'others' othering each other all over the world. Accreditors are 'others' to the certifiers, who are 'others' to those who follow the ISO 9001 management standard, which in turn is the arche-idea for a rational, formal organization. And precisely as with the idea of hyper-organization, the control regime begets more organizations – the legitimate participants in the control regime are standardized organizations and not people. The control regime can, in addition, be regarded as hyper-organization because everything handled in the control regime's activities, the actual raw material of the control regime, has to do with organizing: making decisions, deciding on decisions and organizing the organizations. It is not about child care, farming or testing physical products.

The concept of hyper-organization thus helps to describe the control regime as a phenomenon, and this could explain why this organizing occurs in the first place – the control regime becomes an expression of a rationalized society and the organizations in the control regime are the answer to the rational environment. The argument put forward by Bromley and Meyer (2015) places organizations back in the center of the new institutionalism. But organization is still assumed to be an order reserved for the formal organization – everything else outside of it becomes the rational environment. This also means that the concept of hyper-organization cannot fully explain how the control regime is composed and what actually holds it together. With regard to the theoretical question of how the construction and the assembling of the control regime can be understood, through all of the organizations and all of the organizing among them, hyper-organization does not tell the whole story.

THE CONTROL REGIME AND FORMAL ORGANIZATION

In my analysis of the control regime I described how I turned the idea of formal organization inside-out to show that the principles of organizing that exist within organizations are also found outside them. I then showed that the control regime contains all of the traditional organization principles that Weber and Fayol, among others, have used to describe organization as a kind of social order. Does this mean that if I then turn things back the other way and put all the parts of the control regime together into a single whole, that I will simply get a formal organization again?

That the control regime is composed of a number of interchangeable organizations can be likened to how formal organizations are made up of members that can be interchanged without the organization ceasing to exist. And precisely as inside an organization, there is, within the control regime, a division of labor, coordination, formalization, and a hierarchy. All of the organizational elements (Ahrne and Brunsson 2011) – rules, hierarchy, sanctions, control and membership – can also be found in the control regime. Just like the formal organization, it has a rational, composite inside, with a hierarchical structure (Meyer and Bromley 2013; Bromley and Sharkey 2017).

As an organizational phenomenon, the control regime is actually strikingly similar to a formal organization. The control regime as an organized state of being is so similar to a formal organization that to refer to it as 'the environment' or 'a network' would be misleading. The control regime is too organized for that.

But several aspects also make the control regime different from the formal organization. In the control regime there is no central decision-maker. And, as opposed to the formal organization depicted as a social actor (Meyer 2010) that is expected to act and make decisions of one's own, the control regime is not able to act. The control regime has no interests, the control regime cannot choose among alternatives, the control regime as a whole has no identity, no sovereignty and no autonomy. Neither is the control regime a formal organization in the sense of a legal person – the control regime is not registered anywhere, the control regime has no name and no physical address, you cannot visit the control regime and you cannot take it to court. Since the control regime is not a legal person or a social actor, neither can the control regime be assigned responsibility. The members that make up a formal organization can ideally hold the organization to account if they feel they have been mistreated. But the control regime is not something one can become a member of because the control regime is not a physical or legal place. The interchangeable organizations are not members, but rather cogs without rights.

The control regime is an organized state, constructed like an organization but with no clear responsibility that can be localized within the control regime or assigned to the control regime as a whole. The control regime cannot be held to account, because you cannot contact the control regime. It is a faceless organizational phenomenon with all of the attributes of a formal organization but none of its obligations. Understanding the control regime as an organized phenomenon of its own means the dichotomy between organizations and environment ultimately disappears – the 'environment' surrounding the organizations is at *least* as organized as the organizations, which is why the boundary between organizations and their environment becomes porous, fluid and relative.

MACRO-ORGANIZATION

I have now looked at different ways of understanding the organizing among and outside organizations presented in contemporary organization theory. I have shown in the book that this happens – the entire control regime is an empirical phenomenon the composition of which can be understood as a specific form of organizing among organizations. But I still lack a concept for understanding the phenomenon that arises when all of the components of the regime – all of the organizations and all of the organizing principles – are put together into a single whole. A whole built of organization and that breeds more organization.

This, I call macro-organization (see also Brunsson, Gustafsson and Tamm-Hallström 2018). Macro-organization is not to be understood as a metaphysical concept, where the whole is larger than the sum of its parts. Macro-organization is a concept by which to understand contemporary organizing, perhaps above all global organizing. A phenomenon that stretches across national borders, geographical boundaries and analytical limits between organizations and their environment. Macro-organization is the result of a belief that organization is the solution to most types of problems, not least the problems of globalization. There seems, in addition, to be a tendency to try to solve organizational problems with more organization. Macro-organization is populated by organizations and not people, its sole purpose being to organize organization. This makes macro-organization universal; it builds on values such as rationality and systematics that are assumed today to be viable in all settings, regardless of tradition or cultural context.

Macro-organization is an expression of an order that is larger than any singular body would be able to monitor and control or take responsibility for. My attempt to understand how organizations and organizing principles are brought together into a sort of organized whole, is highly reminiscent of Callon and Latour's comparison to the Leviathan (1981), where the interconnection of the different parts fuses into something bigger, into a macro-actor. Macro-actors can be organizations or conglomerates. Callon and Latour's concept is above all another way to study organizing, to not assume that the organization exists, ready and waiting to be observed. The organization comes into being through all of the connections and translations that it is composed of, a perspective I presented in Chapter 3. But, as opposed to Callon and Latour's macro-actor, macro-organization is not an actor. The fact that macro-organization is not an actor and therefore not able to act, is what distinguishes macro-organization from formal organization and macro-actors. The lack of agency may be the most important implication of the phenomenon of macro-organization.

MACRO-ORGANIZATION AND AGENCY

There are two ways to discuss agency in relation to macro-organization: agency of the parts that together make up the greater whole, and agency of the greater whole.

The agency of the organizations that together make up macro-organization is both created and circumscribed by them being parts of a larger whole. One of the premises for participating in the control regime is to be an organization, and included in that are the characteristics attributed to it as such – among other things, the expectation that it will act and make decisions about itself or those which the specific organization is assigned to decide over (accreditation over certification for example). In that sense, the control regime distributes actorhood among the organizations participating. But interpreting organizations as interchangeable tools rather than autonomous entities serves to circumscribe their agency and the distributed actorhood – they can only act within the limits of their specific function. In other words, an organization's place in macro-organization both provides agency and at the same time restricts it.

Since macro-organization is not an actor, not an entity, macro-organization cannot act as a whole. Even if, as a phenomenon, macro-organization is built on explicit organizing efforts between the parts, there are no decisions that apply for the entire macro-organization, there is no 'constitution' in macro-organization. There could not be one, because there is no central controlling function in macro-organization, no one to write such a constitution. This means that, as a whole, macro-organization can never be held to account for anything, be asked to take responsibility for anything, or be expected to act on anything. Macro-organization might be extremely assembled but it lacks agency. Macro-organization is an enormous organizational, composite whole without agency, and without the ability to take responsibility. These characteristics are macro-organization's most prominent and perhaps most important implications.

WHO IS AN 'OTHER'?

How are we supposed to trust products, people and organizations in a global world? I started the book by asking how consumers are to reduce uncertainty about the things that they buy and the organizations that surround them. I have now shown how an order was constructed over the course of more than 40 years to solve the problem of uncertainty and distance that arises as our world becomes global – a complex order where no-one controls but where everyone is controlled, where everyone has some responsibility but no-one is responsible for everything.

Does the control regime reduce consumers' uncertainty? The answer to this is naturally individual, and varies from person to person. But I think it is safe to say that the control regime seems to come with a strong belief that organization can solve many problems. Organization – both within and outside organizations – becomes the 'other.' Organization becomes what people are to trust instead of trusting each other. Organization becomes the God, king, or universal controller that people are to believe in, to guide them (Brunsson 2007). Organization replaces the lack of human contact. If the original problem was people's inability, in a global world, to be in direct contact with each other, the control regime has not solved the problem. In order to reduce uncertainty, consumers and citizens are instead in contact with a dense and complex state of organization. And a faceless one. No-one can communicate with the control regime as a whole. It has no name or address. Although, it seems evident that we need an 'other,' an authority to guide us. When the American philosopher Richard Rorty wrote that 'the pragmatists' anti-representationalist account of belief is, among other things, a protest against the idea that human beings must humble themselves before something non-human, whether the Will of God or the Intrinsic Nature of Reality' (2006: 257), the type of organization that the control regime represents could be an example of yet another power or authority that people 'humble themselves before,' that they turn to in search of truth and meaning. The rationality sought by the control regime has replaced a religious conviction of safety for human existence. In many ways, the control regime describes how religion has been replaced by rationality. Or one could even say that the belief in rationality and the organizational expression of it, is the religion of today: the idea that organization will solve everything is religious in its conviction, but packed and sealed as scientism, individualism and securalism.

MACRO-ORGANIZATION AS AN 'ORGANIZED OTHER'

At the beginning of this book, I asked who someone else, an 'other,' was. An 'other' can be interpreted in practical, concrete terms – for example, as a third party in the form of a certification company that assesses things instead of the consumer doing it him/herself. But an 'other' can also be understood more abstractly, or phenomenologically. In this book I have shown how macro-organization as an organized state of being constitutes an 'other,' someone or something that is not 'you' or 'I.' At the same time macro-organization absorbs all forms of alterity and differentness, everything that is different from the masses. People's uncertainty and need for control guide them to reduce the 'other', the 'other' is incorporated into the already known. But the differentness cannot be classified and reduced, because it then disappears and with it, the possibility to challenge, question and develop oneself, the 'I' (Kemp 1992). It is in the reflection of others that people and organizations come to exist (Mead 1934) – not by the reduction, classification and organization of the 'other.' By organizing differentness into a rationalized, collective whole, into that which people already are and know, everything becomes the same. Systemized, standardized and interchangeable.

Earlier I described how Meyer (2010) discusses organizations that organize other organizations as a kind of 'others.' As a composite phenomenon of both organization and organizations, macro-organization as a whole can be understood as a single big 'organized other,' where all forms of differentness in the form of cultural tradition and local uniqueness are organized out of existence. A society full of such absorbing organization becomes self-reinforcing – more and more organizations are created to justify and organize more and more organizations in a continually ongoing process.

So how is this to continue? Should the control regime be terminated or discontinued? To borrow Gustafsson's (1994) expression, it would seem that organization is surrounded by a 'wall of indisputability'; organization seems to be the answer to most things without actually having been questioned. Organization signals a kind of science and rationality from which authority and indisputability can be drawn. And if we are to question or change a rule or other part of the organization this is best done by writing a new rule to complement or amend the old one. That organization and standardization appear to be incontrovertible and represent some sort of universal 'truth' about how to do things right, results in the non-standardized appearing less true. Interpersonal trust becomes an abstract idea that can't be measured, intuition becomes 'new-age drivel' that cannot be documented according to specified requirements, while differences are positive only within the limits of differences should behave.

There is no room for the 'other.'

Guillet de Monthoux (1981) wrote about standards early on and pondered where this (all too) eager rule-creating would end. He pointed out that the idea of standards and standardization – as all other regulation – was founded on normative ideas of how something *should* be rather than how it actually is. Discontinuation of the control regime would only be possible, as Guillet de Monthoux described it, if we were to really face the fact that there are things that *cannot* be regulated, that *not* everything can be controlled. The control regime cannot be dismantled or avoided with the same materials it was built with. Dismantling of the control regime would require us to return to the state of human trust, the lack of which the control regime lives off.

If an 'other' is an organized, faceless state, what do people become to each other when so much trust is placed in organization, something beyond them?

Do they become like the people in Whyte's *Organization Man* (1956), their lives, dreams and ideas shaped and controlled by organizations? Where organizations take on the role of what to believe in, where religion is replaced by rationality? Do people become like the Japanese soldier Onoda in Guillet de Monthoux's book (1981), a soldier left behind enemy lines in World War II with orders to never surrender unless he heard the agreed-upon signal from his commanding officer. Onoda could never trust who his superiors were, he neither saw them nor heard them. What if he was tricked, what if the signal to surrender came from the enemy? For 30 years, Onoda remained loyal, fighting a war in the jungle, disconnected from reality where peace had long since been established. He never questioned to stop. A loyalty that in no way fits with an individualized, liberated society made up of enlightened, thinking people, and a loyalty that is the opposite of Richard Rorty's thinking, reflective 'ironist.'

Does the control regime create a faceless society detached from reality, that exists to organize more organization, where organizations are standardized and interchangeable but powerful and bear no responsibility, where people obey organizations instead of seeing, listening and talking to one another? Or are we to believe a different, less dystopian picture, like that offered by Shirky (2008), for example, where this era of the internet, globalization and disappearing borders is a time where people organize themselves anyway, without organizations but with each other? More research is needed to answer these questions.

Appendix

DOCUMENTS AND MODULES

Table A.1   Public documents Chapter 4

Resolution 85/C 136/01	*Council resolution of 7 May 1985 on a new approach to technical harmonization and standards*
COM (89) final – SYN 208	*A global approach to certification and testing*
Resolution 90/C 10/01	*Council Resolution of 21 December 1989 on a global approach to conformity assessment (90/C 10/01)*
Proposition 1991/92:170 (Annex 11)	*om Europeiska ekonomiska samarbetsområdet (EES) (Proposition about the European Economic Cooperation)*
SFS 1992:1534	*Lag om CE-märkning (Law on the CE mark)*
SFS 1992:1119	*Lag om teknisk kontroll (Law in technical assessment)*
Proposition 1992/93:87	*om en ny lag om EG-märket (Proposition on a new law about the EG mark)*
Beslut 93/465/EEC	*Rådets beslut av den 22 juli 1993 om moduler för olika stadier i förfaranden vid bedömning av överensstämmelse samt regler för anbringande och användning av EG-märkning om överensstämmelse, avsedda att användas i tekniska harmoniseringsdirektiv (Council Decision of July 22, 1993 concerning the modules for the various phases of the conformity assessment procedures and the rules for the affixing and use of the CE conformity marking, which are intended to be used in the technical harmonization directives)*
Proposition 1993/94:161	*Marknadskontroll för produktsäkerhet m m. (Proposition on market surveillance and product safety)*
Proposition 1997/98:136	*Statlig förvaltning i medborgarnas tjänst (Proposition on a public administration in the service of citizens)*

Europaparlamentets och rådets direktiv 98/34/EC	*om ett informationsförfarande beträffande tekniska standarder och föreskrifter (Directive 98/34/EC of the European Parliament and of the Council of June 22, 1998 laying down a procedure for the provision of information in the field of technical standards and regulations)*
Dir. 2003:34	*Översyn av marknadskontrollens framtida organisation och finansiering (Oversight of the future market surveillence organization)*
SOU 2004:57	*Tillsyn för säkra varor och öppna marknader (Surveillance of safe goods and open markets)*
Proposition 2004/05:98	*Riktlinjer för marknadskontroll av produkter m.m. (Proposition on guidelines for market surveillence of goods)*
SFS 2005:893	*Förordning om marknadskontroll av varor (Regulation on market surveillence of goods)*
Dir. 2005:138	*Översyn av det öppna systemet för provning och teknisk kontroll (Oversight of the open system of testing and technical assessments)*
SOU 2006:113	*Öppna system för provning och kontroll – en utvärdering (An open system for testing and control – an evaluation)*
Regeringens skrivelse 2007/08:140	*Standardiseringens betydelse i en globaliserad värld (The impact of standardization in a global world)*
SOU 1989:45	*Standardiseringens roll I EF/EFTA samarbetet*

Table A.2   Public documents Chapter 5

Europaparlamentets och rådets Förordning 764/2008/EG	*om förfaranden för tillämpning av vissa nationella tekniska regler på produkter som lagligen saluförts i en annan medlemsstat och om upphävande av beslut nr 3052/95/EG (Regulation (EC) no 764/2008 of the European Parliament and of the Council of July 9, 2008 laying down procedures relating to the application of certain national technical rules to products lawfully marketed in another Member State and repealing Decision No 3052/95/EC)*
Europaparlamentets och rådets förordning 765/2008/EG	*om krav på ackreditering och marknadskontroll i samband med saluföring med produkter och upphävande av förordning (EEG) nr 339/93 (Regulation (EC) no 765/2008 of the European Parliament and of the Council of July 9, 2008 setting out the requirements for accreditation and market surveillance relating to the marketing of products and repealing Regulation (EEC) No 339/93)*

Europaparlamentets och rådets beslut 768/2008/EG	*om en gemensam ram för saluföring av produkter och upphävande av rådets beslut 93/465/EEG (Decision No 768/2008/EC of the European Parliament and of the Council of July 9, 2008 on a common framework for the marketing of products, and repealing Council Decision 93/465/EEC)*
Blue Guide version 1.1.	*Om genomförandet av EU:s produktbestämmelser (Implementation of the EU product regulations)*
Proposition 2010/11:80	*Ny lag om ackreditering och teknisk kontroll (Proposition on a new law for accreditation and technical assessment)*
EA 2/02 2011	*EA Procedure for the evaluation of a National Accreditation Body*
BIS 2011	*The Accreditation Logo and Symbols: Conditions for use by UKAS and UKAS accredited organizations*
UKAS program proposal 2011–14	*UKAS Awareness Campaign*
SFS 2011:791	*Lag om ackreditering och teknisk kontroll (Law on accreditation and technical assessment)*
Ds. 2013:12	*Marknadskontroll av varor och annan närliggande tillsyn (Market surveillance of goods and other related surveillance practices)*
SFS 2014:1039	*Förordning om marknadskontroll av varor och annan närliggande tillsyn (Law on market surveillance and other related surveillance practices)*

www.iaf.nu

www.european-accreditation.org

www.swedac.se

www.konsumentverket.se

MODULES IN THE GLOBAL APPROACH

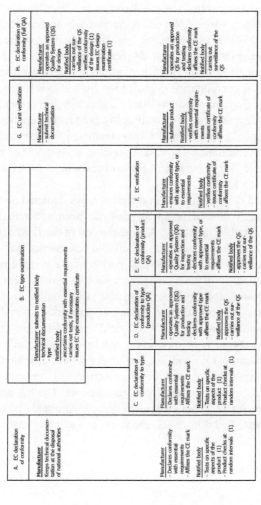

CONFORMITY ASSESSMENT PROCEDURES IN COMMUNITY LEGISLATION

A. EC declaration of conformity

DESIGN

Manufacturer
Keeps technical documentation at the disposal of national authorities

PRODUCTION

Manufacturer
- Declares conformity with essential requirements
- Affixes the CE mark

Notified body
- Tests on specific aspects of the product (1)
- Product checks at random intervals (1)

B. EC type examination

Manufacturer submits to notified body
- type
- technical documentation

Notified body
- ascertains conformity with essential requirements
- carries out tests, if necessary
- issues EC type-examination certificate

C. EC declaration of conformity to type

Manufacturer
- Declares conformity with essential requirements
- Affixes the CE mark

Notified body
- Tests on specific aspects of the product (1)
- Product checks at random intervals (1)

D. EC declaration of conformity to type (production QA)

Manufacturer
- operates an approved Quality System (QS) for production and testing
- declares conformity with approved type
- affixes the CE mark

Notified body
- approves the QS
- carries out surveillance of the QS

E. EC declaration of conformity (product QA)

Manufacturer
- operates an approved Quality System (QS) for inspection and testing
- declares conformity with approved type, or to essential requirements
- affixes the CE mark

Notified body
- approves the QS
- carries out surveillance of the QS

F. EC verification

Manufacturer
- ensures conformity with approved type, or to essential requirements

Notified body
- verifies conformity
- issues certificate of conformity
- affixes the CE mark

G. EC unit verification

Manufacturer
- submit technical documentation

Manufacturer
- submits product

Notified body
- verifies conformity with essential requirements
- issues certificate of conformity
- affixes the CE mark

H. EC declaration of conformity (full QA)

Manufacturer
- operates an approved Quality System (QS) for design

Notified body
- carries out surveillance of the design (1)
- verifies conformity of the design (1)
- issues EC design examination certificate (1)

Manufacturer
- operates an approved QS for production and testing
- declares conformity
- affixes the CE mark

Notified body
- carries out surveillance of the QS

(1) supplementary requirements which may be used in specific directives

Figure A.1   The modules in the global approach (COM (89) final – SYN 208:88)

Note on methodology

To study the global control regime, I conducted 26 interviews in total, nine of the interviewees were employees at the Swedish accreditation organization *Swedac*. The other interviewees came from different parts of the control regime and were selected in order to provide pictures and stories of those respective parts: representatives from certification companies, representatives from IAF, EA, the UK accreditation organization (in addition to the Swedish one), representatives from market surveillance authorities, a representative from the business organization of toys as well as toy producers (representing the 'economic operators' in the regime). I also conducted five observations in total: three World Accreditation Days, one meeting with the Market Surveillance Council, and one 3-day course on CE marking for toys. All of the observations took place in Stockholm.

I also studied documents that in different ways depicted and described the control regime. Accreditation in Sweden has been and remains an activity carried out by a public authority. A large portion of the field data dealing with accreditation is therefore made up of official documents that are public, not classified. The texts covering the first period of the control regime's development are primarily official documents such as government bills, ministry memoranda, committee directives, administrative regulations or official government reports. As accreditation became organized more and more through EU or international organizations my field data collection came to include also other sources such as directives, regulations and guidance documents from the EU Commission and EU Parliament. I have also studied documents from industry associations, member organizations of the accreditation organizations, the EU and standardization organizations. The EA and the IAF also publish documents (e.g. policies, guidelines, memoranda of understanding), which I have analysed. I have also made use of the information on the EA and IAF websites.

References

Abbot, K. W., Levi-Faur, D. and Snidal, D. (2017). Theorizing regulatory intermediaries: the RIT model. *The Annals of American Political and Social Science*. AAPSS 670 March 2017.

Abbott, K. W. and Snidal, D. (2009). The governance triangle: regulatory standards institutions and the shadow of the state (pp. 44–88), in Mattli, W. and Woods, N. (eds.), *The Politics of Global Regulation*. Princeton: Princeton University Press.

Ahrne, G. and Brunsson, N. (2011). Organization outside organizations: the significance of partial organization. *Organization*, 18 (1): 83–104.

Ahrne, G. and Brunsson, N. (2019). *Organization Outside Organizations. The Abundance of Partial Organization in Social Life*. Cambridge: Cambridge University Press.

Ahrne, G., Brunsson, N. and Seidl, D. (2016). Resurrecting organizations by going beyond organizations. *European Management Journal*, 34 (2): 93–101.

Apelt, M., Besio, C., Corsi, G., Groddeck, V., von, Grothe-Hammer, M. and Tacke, V. (2017). Resurrecting organization without renouncing society: a response to Ahrne, Brunsson and Seidl. *European Management Journal*, 35: 8–14.

Bartley, T. (2007). Institutional emergence in an era of globalization: the rise of transnational private regulation of labor and environmental conditions. *American Journal of Sociology*, 113 (2): 297–351.

Bartley, T. (2010). Transnational private regulation in practice: the limits of forest and labor standards certification in Indonesia. *Business and Politics*, 12 (3): Article 7.

Bartley, T. (2011). Certification as a mode of social regulation (pp. 441–452), in Levi-Faur, D. (ed.), *Handbook on the Politics of Regulation*. Cheltenham, UK and Northampton, MA, USA: Edward Elgar Publishing.

Bartley, T. and Smith, S N. (2010). Communities of practices as cause and consequence of transnational governance: the evolution of social and environmental certification (pp. 347–374), in Djelic M.L. and Quack, S. (eds.), *Transnational Communities: Shaping Global Economic Governance*. Cambridge: Cambridge University Press.

Beck, N. and Walgenbach, P. (2005). Technical efficiency or adaptation to institutionalized expectations? The adoption of ISO 9000 standards in the German mechanical engineering industry. *Organization Studies*, 26 (6): 841–866.

Bernstein, S. and Cashore, B. (2007). Can non-state global governance be legitimate? An analytical framework. *Regulation and Governance*, 1 (4): 1–25.

Besen, S. M. and Farrell, J. (1994). Choosing how to compete: strategies and tactics in standardization. *The Journal of Economic Perspectives*, 8 (2): 117–131.

Blau, P. (1968). The hierarchy of authority in organizations. *American Journal of Sociology*, 73 (4): 453–467.

Boiral, O. (2012). ISO certificates as organizational degrees? Beyond the rational myths of the certification process. *Organization Studies*, 33 (5–6): 633–654.

Boström, M. (2006). Regulatory credibility and authority through inclusiveness: standardization organizations in cases of eco-labeling. *Organization*, 13 (3): 345–367.

Boström, M. and Tamm Hallström, K. (2010). NGO power in global social and environmental standard setting. *Global Environmental Politics*, 10 (4): 36–59.

Bromley, P. and Meyer, J. W. (2015). *Hyper-Organization: Global Organizational Expansion*. Oxford: Oxford University Press.

Bromley, P. and Sharkey, A. (2017). Casting call. The expanding nature of actorhood in US firms 1960–2010. *Accounting, Organization and Society*, 59: 3–20.

Brunsson, N. (1985). *The Irrational Organization. Irrationality as a Basis for Organizational Action and Change*. Chichester: Wiley.

Brunsson, N. (1989). *The Organization of Hypocrisy: Talk, Decisions and Actions in Organizations*. Chichester: Wiley.

Brunsson, N. (2007). *The Consequences of Decision-making*. Oxford: Oxford University Press.

Brunsson, N. and Jacobsson, B. (2000). *A World of Standards*. Oxford: Oxford University Press.

Brunsson, N. and Jutterström, M. (eds.) (2018). *Organizing and Reorganizing Markets*. Cambridge: Cambridge University Press.

Brunsson, N. and Sahlin-Andersson, K. (2000). Constructing organizations: the case of public sector reform. *Organization Studies*, 21 (4): 721–746.

Brunsson, N., Gustafsson, I. and Tamm Hallström, K. (2018). Market, trust and the construction of macro-organizations (pp. 136–152), in Brunsson, N. and Jutterström, M. (eds.), *Organizing and Reorganizing Markets*. Cambridge: Cambridge University Press.

Brunsson, N., Rasche, A. and Seidl, D. (2012). The dynamics of standardization: three perspectives on standards in organization studies. *Organization Studies*, 33 (5–6): 613–632.

Callon, M. and Latour, B. (1981). Unscrewing the big Leviathan (pp. 277–303), in Knorr-Cetina, K. and Cicourel, A. V. (eds.), *Advances in Social Theory and Methodology. Toward an Integration of Micro and Macro-Sociologies*. Boston, London and Henley: Routledge and Kegan Paul.

Conroy, M. E. (2007). *Branded! How the Certification Revolution is Transforming Global Corporations*. Gabriola Island: New Society Publishers.

Corvellec, H. and Czarniawska, B. (2014). *Action Nets for Waste Prevention*. GRI Report. No 2014:1.

Corvellec, H., Ek, R., Zapata, P. and Zapata Campos, M. J. (2016). Acting on distances: a topology of accounting inscriptions. *Accounting, Organization and Society*, 67: 56–65.

Crozier, M. (1964). *The Bureaucratic Phenomenon*. Chicago and London: University of Chicago Press.

Cutler, C., Haufler, V. and Porter, V. (eds.) (1999). *Private Authority and International Affairs*. Albany: State University of New York Press.

Czarniawska, B. (2004). On time, space and action nets. *Organization*, 11 (6): 773–791.

Czarniawska, B. (2010). Going back to go forward: on studying organizing in action nets (pp. 140–160), in Hernes, T. and Maitlis, S. (eds.), *Process, Sensemaking and Organizing*. Oxford: Oxford University Press.

Czarniawska, B. (2013). Organizations as obstacles to organizing (pp. 3–22), in Robichaud, D. and Cooren, F. (eds.), *Organization and Organizing. Materiality, Agency, and Discourse*. New York: Routledge.

Djelic, M. L. and Sahlin-Andersson, K. (eds.) (2006). *Transnational Governance: Institutional Dynamics of Regulation*. Cambridge: Cambridge University Press.

Drori, G., Höllerer, M. and Walgenbach, P. (2014). Unpacking the glocalization of organization: from term, to theory, to analysis. *European Journal of Cultural and Political Sociology*, 1 (1): 85–99.

Drori, G., Jang, S. Y. and Meyer, J. W. (2006). Sources of rationalized governance: cross-national longitudinal analyses, 1985–2002. *Administrative Science Quarterly*, 51 (2): 205–229.

Drori, G., Meyer, J. W. and Hwang, H. (2006). *Globalization and Organization. World Society and Organizational Change.* Oxford: Oxford University Press.

du Gay, P. (2000). *In Praise of Bureaucracy. Weber, Organization, Ethics.* London: Sage.

Erlingsdottir, G. and Lindberg, K. (2005). Isomorphism, isopraxism and isonymism: complementary or competing processes? (pp. 47–70), in Czarniawska, B. and Sévon, G. (eds.), *Global Ideas: How Ideas, Objects and Practices Travel in the Global Economy.* Copenhagen: Liber and CBS Press.

Farrell, J. and Saloner, G. (1988). Coordination through committees and markets. *The RAND Journal of Economics*, 19 (2): 235–252.

Fayol, H. (1916/2008). *Industriell och allmän administration*, translation Holmblad Brunsson, K. 2008. Stockholm: Santérus Förlag.

Feng, P. (2003). *Studying Standardization: A Review of the Literature 2003:99.* SIIT 2003 Conference proceedings. IEEE.

Fjeldstad, O. D., Snow, C. C., Miles, R. E. and Lettl, C. (2012). The architecture of collaboration. *Strategic Management Journal*, 33 (6): 734–750.

Foucault, M. (1975/1987). *Övervakning och straff. Fängelsets födelse.* Lund: Arkiv förlag.

Fouilleux, E. and Loconto, A. (2016). Voluntary standards, certification, and accreditation in the global organic agriculture field: a tripartite model of techno-politics. *Agriculture and Human Values*, 1–14.

Frankel, C. and Hojbjerg, E. (2007). The constitution of a transnational policy field: negotiating the EU internal market for products. *Journal of European Public Policy*, 14 (1): 97–115.

Friedland, R. and Alford, R. R. (1991). Bringing society back in: symbols, practices and institutional contraindications (pp. 232–263), in Powell, W. W. and DiMaggio, P. J. (eds.), *The New Institutionalism in Organizational Analysis.* Chicago: University of Chicago Press.

Gilbert, D. U. and Rasche, A. (2007). Discourse ethics and social accountability: the ethics of SA 8000. *Business Ethics Quarterly*, 17 (2): 187–216.

Guillet de Monthoux, P. (1981). *Dr Kant och den oekonomiska rationaliseringen. Om det normativas betydelse för företagens, industrins och teknologins ekonomi.* Göteborg: Korpen.

Gustafsson, C. (1994). *Produktion av allvar.* Stockholm: Nerenius och Santérus förlag.

Gustafsson, I. and Tamm Hallström, K. (2013). The certification paradox: monitoring as a solution and a problem (pp. 91–110), in Reuter, M., Wijkström, F. and Kristensson Uggla, B. (eds.), *Trust and Organizations. Confidence Across Borders.* New York: Palgrave.

Gustafsson, I. and Tamm Hallström, K. (2018). Hyper-organized eco-labels: an organization studies perspective on the implementation of tripartite standards regimes. *Food Policy*, 75: 124–133.

Hall, R. (1963). The concept of bureaucracy: an empirical assessment. *American Journal of Sociology*, 69 (1): 32–40.

Hatanaka, M. (2010). Governing sustainability: examining audits and compliance in a third-party-certified organic shrimp farming project in rural Indonesia. *Local Environment*, 15 (3): 233–244.

Hatanaka, M. (2014). Standardized food governance? Reflections on the potential and limitations of chemical-free shrimp. *Food Policy*, 45: 138–145.

Hatanaka, M. and Busch, L. (2008). Third-party certification in the global agrifood system: an objective or socially mediated governance mechanism? *Sociologica Ruralis*, 48 (1): 73–91.

Hatanaka, M., Konefal, J. and Constance, D. H. (2012). A tripartite standards regime analysis of the contested development of a sustainable agriculture standard. *Agriculture and Human Values*, 29 (1): 65–78.

Haufler, V. (2001). A public role for the private sector: industry self-regulation in a global economy. *Carnegie Endowment for International Peace*, Washington: Brookings Institution Press.

Haufler, V. (2003). New forms of governance: certification regimes as social regulations of the global market (pp. 237–247), in Meidinger, E., Elliott. C. and Oesten, G. (eds.), *Social and Political Dimensions of Forest Certification*. Remagen-Oberwinter: Kessel.

Hernes, T. (2007). *Understanding Organization as Process. Theory for a Tangled World*. London: Routledge.

Higgins, W. and Tamm Hallström, K. (2007). Standardization, globalization and rationalities of government. *Organization*, 14 (5): 685–704.

ISO Survey 2017 (www.iso.org).

Jacobsson, B. (1993). Europeiseringen av förvaltningen. *Statsvetenskaplig Tidskrift*, 96 (2): 113–137.

Jacobsson, B., Pierre, J. and Sundström G. (2015). *Governing the Embedded State. The Organizational Dimension of Governance*. Oxford: Oxford University Press.

Jepperson, R. (1991). Institutions, institutional effects and institutionalism (pp. 143–163), in Powell, W. W. and DiMaggio, P. J. (eds.), *The New Institutionalism in Organizational Analysis*. Chicago: University of Chicago Press.

Joerges, B. and Czarniawska, B. (1998). The question of technology, or how organizations inscribe the world. *Organization Studies*, 19 (3): 363–385.

Kemp, P. (1992). *Emmanuel Lévinas – en introduktion*. Göteborg: Bokförlaget Daidalos Ab.

Kerwer, D. (2005). Holding global regulators accountable: the case of credit rating agencies. *Governance*, 18 (3): 453–475.

Kouakou, D., Boiral, O. and Gendron, Y. (2013). ISO-auditing and the construction of trust in auditor independence. *Accounting, Auditing & Accountability Journal*, 26 (8): 1279–1305.

Lamoreaux, N. R. (2004). Partnerships, corporations, and the limits on contractual freedom in U.S. history: an essay in economics, law and culture (pp. 2–65), in Lipartito, K. and Sicilia, D. B. (eds.), *Constructing Corporate America: History, Politics, Culture*. Oxford: Oxford University Press.

Lampland, M. and Star, S. (2009). *Standards and Their Stories: How Quantifying, Classifying, and Formalizing Practices Shape Everyday Life*. London: Cornell University Press.

Latour, B. (1987). *Science in Action: How to Follow Scientists and Engineers through Society*. Cambridge, MA: Harvard University Press.

Latour, B. (2005). *Reassembling the Social: An Introduction to Actor-Network-Theory*. Oxford: Oxford University Press.

Law, J. (1986). On methods of long distance control: vessels, navigation, and the Portuguese route to India, in Law, J. (ed.), *Power, Action and Belief: A New Sociology of Knowledge? Sociological Review*, Monograph 32. Henley: Routledge.

Law, J. and Hetherington, K. (2000). Materialities, spatialities, globalities (pp. 34–49), in Bryson, J., Daniels, P., Henry, N. and Pollard, J. (eds.), *Knowledge, Space, Economy*. London: Routledge.

Law, J. and Mol, A. (2008). Globalisation in practice: on the politics of boiling pigswill. *Geoforum*, 39 (1): 133–143.

Law, J. and Singleton, V. (2005). Object lessons. *Organization*, 12 (3): 331–355.

Levi-Faur, D. and Starobin, S. (2013). Transnational politics and policy: from two-way to three-way intersections. *Jerusalem Papers in Regulation and Governance Working Paper No 62*. Jerusalem: The Hebrew University.

Loconto, A. (2017). Models of assurance: diversity and standardization in modes of intermediation. *Annals of the American Political and Social Sciences*, 670 (March): 112–132.

Loconto, A. and Busch, L. (2010). Standards, techno-economic networks and playing fields: performing the global market economy. *Review of International Political Economy*, 17 (3): 507–536.

Loconto, A. and Fouilleux, E. (2014). Politics of private regulation: ISEAL and the shaping of transnational sustainability governance. *Regulation & Governance*, 8 (2): 166–185.

Loconto, A., Stone, J. V. and Busch, L. (2012). Tripartite standards regime. *The Wiley-Blackwell Encyclopedia of Globalization*. Chichester: Wiley.

Loya, T. and Boli, J. (1999). Standardization in the world polity: technical rationality over power (pp. 169–197), in Boli, J. and Thomas, G. (eds.), *Constructing World Culture: International Non-Governmental Organizations Since 1875*. Stanford: Stanford University Press.

Luhmann, N. (2005). The paradox of decision making (pp. 85–106), in Seidl. D. and Becker K. H. (eds.), *Niklas Luhmann and Organization Studies*. Copenhagen: Copenhagen Business School Press.

March, J. and Olsen, J. P. (1976). *Ambiguity and Choice in Organizations*. Bergen: Universitetsförlaget.

March, J. G. and Simon, H. A. (1958/1993). *Organizations*. New York: Wiley.

Marx, A. (2008). Limits to non-state market regulation: a qualitative comparative analysis of the international sport footwear industry and the Fair Labor Association. *Regulation and Governance*, 2 (2): 253–273.

Marx, A. (2010). Global governance and the certification revolution: types, trends and challenges. *Leuven Centre for Global Governance Studies*, Working Paper No 53 November 2010.

Marx, A. (2011). Global governance and the certification revolution: types, trends and challenges (pp. 590–603), in Levi-Faur, D. (ed.), *Handbook on the Politics of Regulation*. Cheltenham, UK and Northampton, MA, USA: Edward Elgar Publishing.

Marx, A. (2013). Varieties of legitimacy: a configurational institutional design analysis of eco-labels. *Innovation: The European Journal of Social Science Research*, 26 (3): 268–287.

Marx, A. (2014). Legitimacy, institutional design and dispute settlement: the case of eco-certification systems. *Globalizations*, 11 (3): 401–416.

144   *How standards rule the world*

Marx, A. and Cuypers, D. (2010). Forest certification as a global environmental governance tool: what is the macro-effectiveness of the Forest Stewardship Council? *Regulation and Governance*, 4 (4): 408–434.
Mead, G. H. (1934). *Mind, Self and Society: From the Standpoint of Social Behaviorism.* Chicago: University of Chicago Press.
Mendel, P. (2006). The making and expansion of international management standards: the global diffusion of ISO 9000 Quality Management Certificates (pp. 137–166), in Drori, G., Meyer, J. W. and Hwang, H. (eds.), *Globalization and Organization. World Society and Organizational Change*. Oxford: Oxford University Press.
Meyer, J. W. (2010). World society, institutional theories, and the actor. *Annual Review of Sociology*, 36: 1–20.
Meyer, J. W. (2014). World society (pp. 317–328), in Holzer, B., Kastner, F. and Werron, T. (eds.), *From Globalization to World Society*. London: Routledge.
Meyer, J. W. and Bromley, P. (2013). The world expansion of 'organization'. *Sociological Theory*, 31 (4): 366–389.
Meyer, J. W. and Rowan, B. (1977). Institutionalized organizations: formal structure as myth and ceremony. *American Journal of Sociology*, 83 (2): 340–363.
Mörth, U. (2006). Soft regulation and global democracy (pp. 119–136), in Djelic, M. L. and Sahlin-Andersson, K. (eds.), *Transnational Governance: Institutional Dynamics of Regulation*. Cambridge: Cambridge University Press.
Ohlsson, Ö. and Rombach, B. (1998). *Res pyramiderna. Om frihetsskapande hierarkier och tillplattningens slaveri*. Stockholm: Svenska förlaget.
Olsen, J. P. (2003). Maybe it's time to rediscover bureaucracy. *Journal of Public Administration Research and Theory*, 16 (1): 1–24.
Perrow, C. (1986). *Complex Organizations. A Critical Essay*. New York: McGraw-Hill.
Perrow, C. (1991). A society of organizations. *Theory and Society*, 20 (6): 725–762.
Powell, W. W. and DiMaggio, P. J. (eds.) (1991). *The New Institutionalism in Organizational Analysis*. Chicago: University of Chicago Press.
Rasche, A. and Seidl, D. (2019). Standards between partial and complete organization (pp. 39–61), in Ahrne, G. and Brunsson, N. (eds.), *Organization Outside Organizations. The Abundance of Partial Organization in Social Life*. Cambridge: Cambridge University Press.
Reinecke, J., Manning, S. and von Hagen, O. (2012). The emergence of a standards market: multiplicity of sustainability standards in the global coffee industry. *Organization Studies*, 33 (5–6): 791–814.
Robertson, R. (1992). *Globalisation. Social Theory and Global Culture*. London: Sage.
Robson, K. (1992). Accounting numbers as 'inscription': action at a distance and the development of accounting. *Accounting, Organizations and Society*, 17 (7): 685–708.
Rombach, B. (1986). *Rationalisering eller prat: kommuners anpassning till en stagnerande ekonomi*. Kommunal ekonomi och organisation. Lund: Doxa.
Rorty, R. (2006). Pragmatism and anti-authoritarianism (pp. 257–266), in Shook, J. R. and Margolis, J. (eds.), *A Companion to Pragmatism*. Malden: Blackwell Publishing.
Rose, N. and Miller, P. (1992). Political power beyond the state: problematics of government. *British Journal of Sociology*, 43 (2): 173–205.
Rosenau, J. N. (2007). Governing the ungovernable: the challenge of a global disaggregation of authority. *Regulation and Governance*, 1 (1): 88–97.
Sandholtz, K. (2012). Making standards stick: a theory of coupled vs. decoupled compliance. *Organization Studies*, 33 (5–6): 655–679.

Scott, J. C. (1998). *Seeing Like a State: How Certain Schemes to Improve the Human Condition Have Failed*. New Haven: Yale University Press.

Seidl, D. (2007). Standard setting and following in corporate governance: an observation-theoretical study of the effectiveness of governance codes. *Organization*, 14 (5): 705–727.

Shirky, C. (2008). *Here Comes Everybody. The Power of Organizing Without Organizations*. New York: The Penguin Press.

Simon., H. A. (1962). The architecture of complexity. *Proceedings of the American Philosophical Society*, 106 (6): 467–482.

Starbuck, W. H. (2003). The origins of organization theory (pp. 143–182), in Tsoukas, H. and Knudsen, C. (eds.), *The Oxford Handbook of Organization Theory. Meta-theoretical Perspectives*. Oxford: Oxford University Press.

Sundström, A. (2011). Framing numbers at a 'distance': intangible performance reporting in a theater. *Journal of Human Resource Costing & Accounting*, 15 (4): 260–278.

Tamm Hallström, K. (2000). *Kampen för auktoritet. Standardiseringsorganisationer i arbete*. Akademisk avhandling. Stockholm: EFI.

Tamm Hallström, K. (2004). *Organizing International Standardization – ISO and the IASC in Quest of Authority*. Cheltenham, UK and Northampton, MA, USA: Edward Elgar Publishing.

Tamm Hallström, K. and Boström, M. (2010). *Transnational Multi-Stakeholder Standardization. Organizing Fragile Non-State Authority*. Cheltenham, UK and Northampton, MA, USA: Edward Elgar Publishing.

Thompson, J. D. (1956). On building an administrative science. *Administrative Science Quarterly*, 1 (1): 102–111.

Timmermans, S. and Epstein, S. (2010). A world of standards but not a standard world: toward a sociology of standards and standardization. *Annual Review of Sociology*, 36: 69–89.

Waldo, D. (1961). Organization theory: an elephantine problem. *Public Administration Review*, 21 (4): 210–225.

Walgenbach, P. (2001). The production of distrust by means of producing trust. *Organization Studies*, 22 (4): 693–714.

Weber, M. (1922/1983). *Ekonomi och samhälle: Förståelsesociologins grunder*, translation Agne Lundqvist (1983). Lund: Argos.

Wedlin, L. (2011). Going global: rankings as rhetorical devices to construct an international field of management education. *Management Learning*, 42 (2): 199–218.

Whyte, H. W. (1956). *The Organization Man*. New York: Simon & Schuster.

Index

accreditation 7, 9–13, 23, 45, 67–9, 106,
108, 116, 119–20, 123, 126
clarification of 67–8
definition of 23–4
and the Global Approach 49–50,
58–60
and global control regime 81–4,
87–9, 92–3, 95–6, 102, 112,
114–15
and Goods Package 67–9, 74
principles of 68–9, 90–91
understanding 26–7
World Accreditation Day 77–9, 93,
96, 114
accreditation organizations 7, 24, 28,
45, 52, 59–60, 76–8, 82–3, 88–9,
91–3, 105, 110, 118–19
see also organizations; Swedac
action nets 33–4
African Accreditation Cooperation 76
Ahrne, G. 33–4, 125
Arab Accreditation Cooperation 76

Bartley, T. 15, 17, 25
Beck, N. 19
behaviorism 32
Blau, P. 32
Blue Guide 61–2, 68–9, 75
Boiral, O. 22
border control 73, 95
Bromley, P. 126–7
Brunsson, N. 4, 13, 17, 33–4, 125
bureaucracy 8, 31–2, 49–50, 81, 86,
101–3, 110–11
definition of 103
through non-bureaucratization
121–2
Busch, L. 14, 16, 21–2, 24, 26

Callon, M. 129
CE mark 53–4, 63–5, 95–7, 100, 106–7,
114, 120
CEN 6, 82–3, 113
CENELEC 6
certification 6–7, 10–13, 20–25, 45, 106,
108, 114–16, 118–19, 123, 125–6
definition of 20–21
and the Global Approach 49, 58–9
and global control regime 81–2, 84,
89, 93, 102, 112
and the New Approach 47
understanding 26–7
certification organizations 6–7, 22–3, 28,
51, 58, 77–8, 83, 88–9
see also organizations; third party
chain-like linkage 85, 89–90, 97–101,
107
child labor 1
confidence 49–50, 74, 91–2
conformity assessment 46, 50–53, 57, 59,
61–3, 65, 67–8, 70, 73–4, 76, 78,
85–89, 91, 94, 105
multilayered 25, 27
control at a distance 28–9, 37–40, 98–99,
102–3
control regime *see* global control regime
Czarniawska, B. 33

Danak 92
Decision 768/2008/EC 62–3, 94–5
decoupling 19
Denmark 92
DiMaggio, P. J. 8
directives 13–14, 46–7, 65, 83, 90, 95,
109, 115
distance 28–9, 36–7, 101
see also control at a distance
different meanings of 106–8
standards and absorption of 108–9